Saints of the English Calendar

Edited by Marcus Holden

and co-written with

Nicholas Schofield, Gerard Skinner, Richard Whinder

ISBN 1-871217-45-8 (hardback)
ISBN 1-871217-46-6 (paperback)

Copyright details for the illustrations
can be found on page iv

The publishers and the authors wish gratefully to acknowledge the assistance provided by all those who helped to locate illustrations for use in this book.

Image editing by Ben Kobus
Cover and page design by Richard Brown

published by
Family Publications
6a King Street
Oxford OX2 6DF
www.familypublications.co.uk

printed by
Cromwell Press, Trowbridge, Wilts.

Saints of the English Calendar

Dedicated to the Most Blessed Virgin Mary,
Our Lady of Walsingham

"For if history records good things of good men,
the thoughtful hearer is encouraged to imitate what is good:
or if it records evil of wicked men, the good, religious listener
or reader is encouraged to avoid all that is sinful and perverse,
and to follow what he knows to be good and pleasing to God."

– St Bede, the first historian of English saints

SOURCES OF ILLUSTRATIONS

Principal Sources: (page numbers refer to this book)

Acta Sanctorum, pro menstrua Patroni sortitione Selectorum, breviter digesta, etc., Fr Daniel Papebroch SJ, two vols., Antwerp, Henri Thieullier, [1694]*
– illustrations on pp. 15, 21, 25, 67, 70, 105, 120, 123, 135

The Flowers of the Lives of the Most Renowned Saincts of the Three Kingdoms England, Scotland and Ireland, vol. 1, Jerome Porter OSB, Douai (really London), 1632*
– frontispiece, illustrations on pp. 7, 33, 36, 39, 43, 53, 61, 91, 109

Other Sources: (page numbers in square brackets refer to this book)

St Aelred of Rievaulx [p. 3] from a drawing of a 12th-century manuscript extracted from the Benedictine Abbey at Anchin (Nord) and now in the Bibliothèque Municipale at Douai.*

Sts Cyril and Methodius [p. 10] from the basilica of San Clemente in Rome.

St David [p. 12] © St Michael's Abbey, Farnborough.

St Anselm [p. 18] from a loose print.*

The English Martyrs [p. 29] from a print, source unknown.

St Columba [p. 47] from a statue in the reredos of St Aloysius' church, Oxford.*

St Richard of Chichester [p. 50] based on a wall painting in the parish church, Black Bourton, Oxon.

St John Fisher from a loose print* and St Thomas More [p. 56] from the frontispiece of *The Life of Sir Thomas More, Kt, Lord High Chancellor of England...*, Thomas More esq. (the saint's great grandson), London, printed for James Woodman and David Lion, 1726.*

St Oliver Plunkett [p. 64] from a painting, courtesy of the Bar Convent Museum, York.

St Teresa Benedicta of the Cross [p. 73] © Edith Stein Archiv, Cologne.

Bl Dominic Barberi [p. 76] from a colour print, courtesy of The Work, Littlemore.

St Margaret Clitherow [p. 80] from illustration facing p. 120 of *Martyrs to the Catholic Faith*, vol. 1, Bishop Challoner, Edinburgh, 1878.*

St Aidan of Lindisfarne [p. 84] from the church of St Aidan, East Acton. Photograph © Fr Nicholas Schofield, 2004.

St Gregory the Great [p. 87] from *Sancti Gregorii Papae I cognomento Magni, Opera Omnia*, vol. 4, Congregation of St Maur, Paris, Claude Rigaud, 1705 (vignette preceding Life of St Gregory by Paul the Deacon).*

St Theodore of Canterbury [p. 95] traced from image found on the internet, source unknown.

Our Lady of Walsingham [p. 98] © St Michael's Abbey, Farnborough.

St Paulinus of York [p. 101] from a window in York Minster, © Sessions Book Trust, York.

St Chad [p. 113] from a drawing of a statue in St Chad's Cathedral, Birmingham, © St Chad's Cathedral, with thanks to the Dean, Fr Brian Doolan.

St Winefride [p. 117] from a statue in her shrine in Holywell.

St Margaret of Scotland [p. 126] from an undated early edition of Butler's *Lives of the Fathers, Martyrs and other Saints*, courtesy of Thicket Priory.

St Hilda [p. 129] by permission of the Principal & Fellows of St Hilda's College, Oxford.

St Hugh of Lincoln [p. 132] © St Michael's Abbey, Farnborough.

St Thomas of Canterbury [p. 138] from a photograph owned by Jerome Bertram CO.*

The publishers gratefully acknowledge the careful and generous assistance provided by Fr Jerome Bertram CO in locating the illustrations marked with an asterisk above, and thank him for allowing their reproduction in this volume.

Proper Calendar for England

FOREWORD

IN LOOKING upon the saints we see Christ. When these saints are men and women from our own land, they manifest in a special way the closeness of the Lord to us.

The timely publication of *Saints of the English Calendar* is an excellent way of getting to know our patrons. I warmly welcome such a great help for all in following the feasts of the new liturgical calendar for England.

I hope this book will have a broad circulation and be a rich source of spiritual reading.

Most Rev. Michael G. Bowen
Archbishop Emeritus of Southwark
4th May, 2004

*I*NTRODUCTION

EVERY CHRISTIAN NATION has its story of how the faith was imparted, took root and flourished; our very national identity is tied up with such a story. England has a particularly rich history of salvation; we are blessed with a great cloud of witnesses across more than 1500 years. The institution of a new and enlarged calendar of saints proper to the Catholic Church in England offers a good opportunity for us to celebrate that history.

The new *Calendarium Proprium*, approved by the Congregation for Divine Worship on 5th June 2000, offers a hugely increased number of over 40 liturgical celebrations proper to England, in which saints from each era of our national story of faith are represented. The patrons of Europe are included, for English Catholic identity was not developed in a vacuum but is intrinsically bound up with the Christian nations of Europe. The patrons of Europe have a special status as obligatory feast days in England and other European countries. Also included are the principal patrons of Ireland, Scotland and Wales, saints invariably linked to English history.

In this book all the saints are arranged according to their date in the national calendar (which is laid out in full at the front of the book) rather than by alphabetical or historical order. The feast of St George has now become a solemnity and therefore the feast of St Adalbert (formerly celebrated on 23rd April in the general calendar) is moved to 24th April in England. Other new features of this calendar include a new feast for all the beatified and canonised martyrs of England on 4th May (which replaces the feast of the 40 martyrs of 30th October) with special celebrations reserved for the Three Women Martyrs (Margaret Clitherow, Anne Line and Margaret Ward) and for Sts John Fisher and Thomas More. The feast of Our Lady of Ransom has become Our Lady of Walsingham.

The Congregation for Divine Worship has also called for the preparation of specific diocesan calendars, which will include variant feasts from the proper calendar. It is hoped that a 'Proper Calendar for Wales' will also be produced – an appendix of Welsh saints is included in this present volume.

I would like to thank everyone who has contributed to the production of this work, especially to my co-writers Nicholas Schofield, Gerard Skinner and Richard Whinder (their particular contributions are indicated by abbreviated initials at the end of each entry: NJS, GS, RW respectively, and MPH for myself).

I hope this work will enable all who read it to come to a greater love and appreciation of our saints and our heritage. It will be a useful reference text also for those who want to know more historically about the saints celebrated in England. It is given primarily, though, as a liturgical and devotional aid both for priests who will celebrate and preach on the feastdays of these saints, and for the faithful who will read and meditate upon the lives of their intercessors; for salvation history is something that continues to go on, and so attention to these saints is not a purely historical curiosity but an acknowledgment of their continuing influence.

Marcus Holden

January 12th
Optional Memorial

St Aelred of Rievaulx

LET him be your storehouse; let Him be your gold purse, your riches and all your delight and pleasure. Let Him be everything to you in all your needs, Who is blessed for ever and ever, Amen.

– St Aelred in his *Letter to My Sister*

THE ENGLISH HAD a close connection with the beginnings of the Cistercian Order, the great monastic movement of the twelfth century. An Englishman, St Stephen Harding, was one of the co-founders of the monastery of Clairvaux and did much to develop the Cistercian constitutions. As third Abbot of Clairvaux, he welcomed St Bernard into the community and appointed him Abbot of Cîteaux at the young age of 24. However, here we are more concerned with the other outstanding English Cistercian of the period: St Aelred of Rievaulx, called the 'Bernard of the North'. If St Bernard was noted for his single-mindedness and sharp wit, whether he was commenting on Holy Writ or preaching the doomed Second Crusade, St Aelred comes across as a warm, conciliatory figure, delighting in the company of his fellow monks, a true 'saint of friendship'.

St Aelred's family takes us back to the local customs of the Northumbrian church, for his father, Eilaf, was hereditary priest of Hexham. The hereditary priesthood, which, by its very nature, meant a married priesthood, was already well into its death throes at the time of St Aelred's birth (1109 AD) due to the reforms started by Pope St Gregory VII. These had been supported by William the Conqueror in return for papal approval for the Norman regime, but caused considerable difficulties in the Northeast. Eilaf was among the last of his breed, and he ended his days as a monk in the new cathedral monastery of St Cuthbert, Durham. Nevertheless, he passed onto his children a love of God and His Church – three of them entered monastic communities.

Eilaf used his contacts with local elites to ensure the best possible education for Aelred, who was eventually sent to the Scottish court of King St David I. Here he became a popular figure, acting as a companion to the heir to the throne, Prince Henry, and being appointed as steward. But such worldly success failed to satisfy Aelred, and he went through a period of restlessness and distress as he tried to discern what life the Lord was asking him to follow. Then, one day in 1134, while he was on official business in Yorkshire, the young man first heard of the newly founded Cistercian abbey of Rievaulx. Staying at a nearby castle, Aelred paid a visit – and was so impressed that the following morning he found himself at the abbey gates begging to be allowed to enter the novitiate.

The world of Rievaulx was very different from the world of the court – but Aelred felt at peace within the austere enclosure and took to the monastic life like a duck to water. In 1142 he was chosen to go to Rome as representative of the Abbot in the controversy surrounding the appointment of the new Archbishop of York, William Fitzherbert, who was accused of simony, impurity and intrusion. However, both the Cistercian abbot's envoy and the prelate whose appointment he was trying to block would one day be venerated as Yorkshire saints. On his return journey from Rome, Aelred stopped off at Clairvaux, and met St Bernard. The great saint did not forget his meeting with this promising young monk, for he was soon chosen as Novice Master and then first Abbot of Revesby. In 1147 he returned to Rievaulx as Abbot. Under his benign rule the community increased to a total number of 650, and the Abbey made five foundations in England and Scotland.

Amidst the busy life of a medieval abbot – domestic administration, lengthy visitations of daughter houses and Chapter meetings at Clairvaux – Aelred found time to compose several spiritual classics, such as his *Spiritual Friendship*, *Mirror of Charity* and a life of St Edward the Confessor. Friendship was at the heart of his spiritual vision, for he was convinced that we are brought to friendship with God through proper human friendships. Though he was thinking primarily of his monks – he called the monastery a 'school of love' – this teaching has a universal value, as valid today as in the twelfth century. 'God Himself is friendship', he said, 'he who dwells in friendship, dwells in God and God in him'. However, we should be careful to avoid self-seeking or purely carnal relationships, for they should always be directed to the Other. St Aelred himself had many friends, including St Godric, possibly a former pirate, who was a famous hermit based at Finchale; and Walter Daniel, his future biographer. His cell was constantly crowded with monks: 'For every day they came to it and sat in it, twenty or thirty at a time, to talk together of the spiritual delights of the Scriptures and of the observance of the Order . . . they walked and lay about his bed and talked with him as a little child prattles with its mother'.

St Aelred suffered from the dreaded kidney stones and spent his last years ruling the Abbey from the Infirmary, where he built himself a special cell. He died on 12th January 1167, surrounded by his community. Never formally canonised, his local cult grew rapidly and his relics were in due course translated from the Chapter House to a new shrine in the abbey church at Rievaulx. The Benedictine historian, Dom David Knowles, has written: 'No other English monk of the twelfth century so lingers in the memory; like [St] Anselm of Bec he escapes from his age, though most typical of it, and speaks directly to us . . . of his restless search for One to whom he might give the full strength of his love'.

NJS

Places to Visit: Rievaulx Abbey itself, set in a picturesque area of the North Yorkshire national park. Despite being a ruin, much of the original structure is preserved as well as the unmistakable atmosphere of tranquillity. Also worth visiting nearby is the nearby sister Abbey of Fountains, the greatest of England's pre-reformation Cistercian houses.

Further Reading:

Anonymous Latin Life of St Ælred by the Bollandists, *Acta Sanctorum*, January, vol. II.

Hallier, A., *The Monastic Theology of Aelred of Rievaulx*, 1969.

Newman, J. H. (ed.), 'St Aelred of Rievaulx', in *Lives of the English Saints*, London, 1845.

Squire, A., *St Ailred of Rievaulx*, 1969.

January 19th
Optional Memorial

St Wulstan

HAPPY is the man who grows sick of the attractions of the world: pleasure of them passes in a moment of time: the tooth of conscience gnaws as long as a man lives.
– St Wulstan (from William of Malmesbury's *Life of St Wulstan*)

WITH THE COMING of William the Conqueror in 1066, we enter into a new period of English history and the story of the nation's faith. The Norman period was marked with the building of great new cathedrals and churches which are still with us today, and by a new interest in learning and scholarship that was to culminate in the founding of the great universities. It was also a time of ecclesiastical reform, organisation and centralisation. That this was achieved without a complete rupture with the past is thanks in no small way to St Wulstan and others like him.

Wulstan was born in 1008, the last years of the Anglo-Saxon period, the time of St Edward the Confessor. Born at Itchington in Warwickshire, he was educated in nearby Evesham. He is no cardboard-cut-out saint, for he was not only renowned in his youth for piety but for the excellence of his sporting prowess. His biographer, Coleman, describes him as being 'of middle height . . . always in good health . . . neither lavish nor niggardly in his choice of clothes and his general standard of living'.

Around 1033 he entered the service of Brihteah, bishop of Worcester. Secular priesthood offered many possibilities of worldly advancement, yet after ordination he declined the offer of a prestigious and wealthy church. He had come to admire the religious life of Worcester Cathedral's Benedictine monks. These he joined and served as sacristan, cantor and schoolmaster. By 1050 he had become prior and began many reforming measures.

In 1062 Aldred bishop of Worcester was appointed to York. After the recommendations of papal legates and the approval of Edward the Confessor and his council, Wulstan was appointed as the diocesan bishop. He made a systematic visitation of his diocese and promoted clerical celibacy, the rebuilding of the Cathedral and of new churches. Although he was a diocesan bishop he remained a monk, living in the monastery and all the while observing the rule. His effective evangelical preaching endeared him to his flock. These were not the signs of a decadent Church at the end of an age.

In 1066, seeing the Norman conquest as an almost inevitable political development, he was one of the first bishops to submit to the Conqueror. Impressed by his reforms, his holiness and his loyalty (particularly during the Barons revolt of 1074–88), Wulstan was allowed by William to remain the only Anglo-Saxon bishop in his See throughout the reign and beyond. This was to provide a smooth transition for his diocese and indeed an example to all wishing to build a successful future. He was no mere opportunist either. His devotion to the Anglo-Saxon saints (particularly to St Bede) was well known, and he propagated this among the Normans until they too acknowledged these patrons as their own. One, St Osmund of Salisbury, despite being a Norman, came to have a great veneration for the Saxon St Aldhelm.

Wulstan himself was impressed and indeed empathised with the reforming spirit of the Norman ecclesiastics. He gave great support to Lanfranc and led his diocese to become a Canterbury suffragan. Wulstan sent his talented disciple Eadmer to the Canterbury school, which further improved the racial and ecclesiastical relationship. He also worked together with the great St Anselm when he succeeded Lanfranc as Archbishop.

Wulstan died in 1095 at the age of 87, the last of his generation of Saxon bishops, having established concord and reform in his diocese and beyond. His cult was an instant success. Many cures and miracles were recorded, especially after 1200. Innocent III officially canonised him in 1203. King John was so devoted to him that, after his death, he was laid to rest close to him.

MPH

Places to Visit: Worcester Cathedral, built around the shrine of Wulstan, still bears something of his memory. In 1218 Bishop Silvester ended an address at the restoration ceremony of the Cathedral after damage by fire with, 'This, dear brethren, is also a place of safety, a port for the tempest-tossed in which the anchorage is sure. Here, by the prayers of priests, men accused of crime may find sure refuge. Venerate therefore the houses of God. Come to them with hearts free from all crime to make offerings of your souls'.

Further reading:

Lamb, J. W., *St Wulfston, Prelate and Patriot*, 1933.

William of Malmesbury, *Life of St. Wulstan*, trans. J.H.F. Peile, Felinfach, Llanerch, 1996.

Mason, E., *St Wulstan of Worcester c.1008–1095*, Oxford, Blackwell, 1990.

February 14th
Feast

Sts Cyril & Methodius

BY the prayers of Mary, almost innumerable sinners are converted.

– St Methodius

WE pray thee, Lord, give us, thy servants, in all time of our life on the earth, a mind forgetful of past ill-will, a pure conscience and sincere thoughts, and a heart to love our brethren; for the sake of Jesus Christ, thy Son, our Lord and only Saviour.

– From the Coptic Liturgy of St Cyril

IN THE ENGLISH CALENDAR these two saints represent the eastern part of European Christendom. They are particularly venerated among the Czechs, Croats, Serbs and Bulgarians. These brothers are the apostles of the Slavs and co-patrons of Europe. They were born in 826 and 815 respectively in Thessalonica, to a senatorial family.

Cyril was called Constantine and educated at the court of Constantinople alongside the young Emperor Michael. He was made librarian at Santa Sophia, and before being ordained he became known as an eminent teacher of philosophy. Methodius was an artist and, in his early days, got involved in politics, as was the family tradition. After some years as a provincial governor he left for the monastic life. In 851, both brothers, being particularly close, went together to a monastery on the Bosphorus.

After a short and successful mission to the Khazars, the two brothers were sent by the Emperor around 863 as missionaries to Moravia (in the modern Czech Republic) at the request of its ruler Rostislav. They were asked to teach in the vernacular tongue, and they translated the scripture and liturgy into Slavonic, inventing thereby the Glagolithic alphabet (from which the 'Cyrillic' was derived later). They are thus considered the founders of Slavonic literature.

At the time of the Photian schism they travelled to Rome after becoming embroiled in a religious/political dispute with German missionaries. Bringing the relics of Pope St Clement I back to Rome, they were well received. Cyril remained in Rome, entering a nearby monastery. He died there in 868 and was buried in the Church of San Clemente, where his relics can be venerated today. In the Church there is a fresco depicting his funeral.

Methodius journeyed back to the mission lands of Moravia, having been made Bishop of Sirmium (Pannonia) by the Pope Hadrian II. He was again opposed by the German missionaries. The great issue was over the use of the vernacular instead of Latin in the liturgy. Methodius stood firm, knowing that the integration of the native people into the faith depended upon this. Eventually his enemies had him thrust into prison. It took Pope John VIII's intervention in 879 and a recall to Rome for official investigation in order to have him released. He was justified in Rome and confirmed as Archbishop of the whole region of Pannonia and Moravia, with full permission for his clergy to celebrate the sacred liturgy in Slavonic. He also completed his translation of the Holy Scriptures into Slavonic.

In 885, after many successful years of evangelisation, Methodius died at Velehrad, and is, with Cyril, the Patron of unity between the Churches of East and West, venerated and loved by both.

MPH

Places to Visit: San Clemente in Rome for the shrine of St Cyril and in Velehrad for that of St Methodius.

Further reading:

Lacko, M., *Sts Cyril and Methodius*, Rome, Pont. Gregorian Univ., 1963.

Tachiaos, A.-E. N., *Cyril and Methodius of Thessalonica: The Acculturation of the Slavs*, St Vladimir's Press, 2001.

Tybor SSCM, Sr. M. M., *Sts Cyril and Methodius, The Glory of the Slavs*, Milwaukee, Catholic Life Publications, Bruce Press, 1953.

March 1st
Feast

ST DAVID

BE joyful, and keep your faith and your creed. Do the little things that you have seen me do and heard about. I will walk the path that our fathers have trod before us.
– The last words of St David

ON THE FAR WESTERN COAST of Britain, in the county of Pembrokeshire, lies the ancient cathedral city of St David. The size of its gothic Cathedral, in comparison to the minute town, is a testimony not only to the priority of the spiritual over the temporal in the medieval world, but to the huge importance this site had for those far beyond the city walls. Pope Callistus II in 1120 had declared two pilgrimages to St David's equal to one to Jerusalem, in terms of the indulgence to be obtained. Yet behind the medieval grandeur and cult there is reflected a devotion to a saint 'Dewi' or 'David' who, in the 6th century, graced those parts with his holy influence, and whose memory is preserved there.

According to tradition, David was born near the present Cathedral on the coast where St Non's chapel now stands. Non is the name of his mother, a noblewoman married to Sant, Prince of Ceredigion. These were Britons, the original people of the island whose existence had been threatened by the fall of the Roman empire and the invasions of the pagan Anglo-Saxons. Their Christianity had probably come through the extension of imperial Rome long before the Gregorian mission of 597.

The earliest life of David is by Rhygyvarch, son of Julien, bishop of St David's around 1090. From this we can glean the core elements behind the hagiographical tradition. He was educated at Henfynw (Aberaeron) but appears to have later moved further afield, coming under the influence of a certain Paulinus, a disciple of St Germanus of Auxerre. After ordination he spent many years on an island studying the scriptures. A legend states that he went on pilgrimage to Jerusalem.

He eventually began to make missionary journeys particularly through south Wales (it is also possible that he went to Brittany). He founded several monasteries including one at Glastonbury and one at Menevia (the place later named St David's), which were known for their strict discipline and austere life modelled on the desert fathers of Egypt. The monks lived off a meagre diet of bread, vegetables and water. These monasteries were self-supporting and therefore required heavy manual labour. Yet at the same time they were seen as great centres of learning and culture. Several Irish saints are said to have been his pupils there. David devoted himself to works of mercy and to mortification. His posthumous nickname of 'Aquaticus' was given him either because he only drank water or because he would immerse himself in freezing water as was the Celtic custom.

At the Synod of Brevi, which was called due to a revival of the native heresy of Pelagianism (Pelagius having come from Britain in the late 4th/early 5th century), David spoke outstandingly against the heresy. He impressed all present. It is said that a white dove descended and rested on his shoulder as he spoke, and is therefore often used in representations of the saint. After this event he was made bishop.

Perhaps due to the encroaching Anglo-Saxons or from a desire for solitude, David soon moved his See from the ancient site of Caerleon to Menevia, where his monastery and his roots lay. The first church was built on the site where the present building now stands by David and his monks. It was here that David died on a Tuesday, the first of March, in the year 589, the monastery having been 'filled with angels as Christ received his soul'.

His cult became very widespread with early church dedications in Brittany, Cornwall and Herefordshire. His relics were translated in 1131, and again in 1275 by Bishop Richard Carew, who re-built the Cathedral from shrine offerings. Kings William I and Henry II visited the shrine. Since the 12th century, David has been regarded as the patron saint of Wales, and is the only Welsh saint to have been venerated in the wider Roman Church. His place in the new English calendar asserts the close ecclesiastical union between England and Wales.

MPH

Places to Visit: The Cathedral of St David and the chapel and house of St Non. The shrine of St Non directly off the Pembrokeshire coast is run by the Passionist fathers and the Sisters of Mercy, and there is a retreat house for pilgrims. Also associated with the cult of St David is Caldey Island off the coast of Tenby, where there are ancient monastic ruins and a living monastery of the Cistercian order.

Further Reading:

Bowen, E. G., *The St David of History. Dewi Sant: Our Founder Saint*, Aberystwyth, The Friends of St David's Cathedral, 1982.

Chadwick, N., *The Age of the Saints in the Early Celtic Church*, Lanerch, 1960.

Doble, G. H., *The Lives of the Welsh Saints*, University of Wales Press, 1991.

James, J. W. (ed.), *Rhygyvarch's Life of St David*, 1967.

March 17th
Feast

St Patrick

CHRIST be in me, Christ be beneath me, Christ be above me, Christ be on my right, Christ be on my left, Christ when I lie down, Christ when I sit down, Christ when I arise, Christ in the heart of everyone who thinks of me, Christ in the mouth of everyone who speaks of me, Christ in every eye that sees me, Christ in every heart that hears me.

– From 'St Patrick's Breastplate'

IN THE FIGURE of St Patrick, history and legend combine to portray a character of immense supernatural charisma with a genius for evangelisation.

Patrick is thought to have been born around the year 390 somewhere in the west of Britain. Whilst still quite young, he was captured by Irish pirates who enslaved him for six years. He was used as a shepherd, possibly in Antrim, during which time he began to pray and underwent a spiritual conversion. One night he had a dream in which he heard the words, 'Soon you will go to your own country.' Being either freed or escaping, Patrick eventually found his way home, where he prepared himself for priesthood.

Contrary to popular belief, Patrick was not the first person to bring the Gospel to Ireland. He succeeded the bishop Palladius, whose mission might not have been very successful. Patrick returned to Ireland after hearing the voice of the Irish calling him back there in his dreams. Having been ordained a bishop, he set up his See at Armagh from where he would travel to spread the Gospel among the Irish.

Patrick's writings are among the first to be identified as authentic from any of the leaders of the Church in the British Isles. These writings, whilst not written in the most refined Latin, show a humble man who had learned through personal trial to trust completely in God.

The many legends that sprang up around the life of St Patrick all bear testimony to a man whom the people remembered with admiration and love, the legends themselves helping to illustrate deep truths about Patrick's life and ministry. An example of this is the famous story of Patrick preaching a sermon about the Trinity on the Hill of Tara. Becoming aware that his congregation could not understand him, he picked up the three-leaved shamrock and used that as a visual aid, the three leaves representing the Father, Son and Holy Spirit, the one plant representing the unity of those three as the one God.

Towards the end of his life, he made a 'retreat' of forty days. The location of this is said to have been on Cruachan Aigli in Mayo, from which the traditional Croagh Patrick pilgrimage derives.

St Patrick is known as the Apostle of the Irish for his ministry and that of his followers after his death, around the year 461. As the patron saint of Ireland, his popularity has spread with the Irish people and missionaries throughout the world, especially to North America and to Great Britain. In art he is usually depicted episcopally attired, driving out the snakes, symbols of evil, from Ireland (as legend tells us), radiant himself with the light of Christ.

GS

Places to Visit: Croagh Patrick, where there is a traditional pilgrimage on the last Sunday of July. Armagh Cathedral marks the site of St Patrick's first See and one can also visit the relics of Patrick at Downpatrick.

Further Reading:

de Breffny, B., *In the Steps of St Patrick*, Thames and Hudson, 1982.

Gallico, P., *The Steadfast Man: A Life of St Patrick*, Four Square, London, 1967.

Hanson, R. P. C., *Saint Patrick: His Origins and Career*, Clarendon Press, 1968.

Kerr, D., *St Patrick*, London, Catholic Truth Society, 1983

O'Loughlin, T., *Saint Patrick, The Man and his Works*, Triangle, 1999.

Shaw, F., *The Real St Patrick,* Dublin, Irish Messenger Office, 1941.

April 21st
Optional Memorial

St Anselm

TEACH me to seek you, and as I seek you, show yourself to me, for I cannot seek you unless you show me how . . .
I do not seek to understand so that I may believe, but I believe so that I may understand.

– From the *Proslogion* of Anselm

THIS DOCTOR OF THE CHURCH was born in the Alpine town of Aosta in 1033. After his beloved mother died in her early years, he was left under the protection of his father with whom he had a very difficult relationship, which culminated in Anselm's leaving home to pursue studies in Burgundy, where his late mother's family lived. After three years he travelled to the monastery of Bec, attracted by the fame of its most illustrious monk, Lanfranc. He entered the community in 1060 and became a fervent disciple of St Benedict. But three years later Lanfranc was appointed Abbot of St Stephen's at Caen – the newly founded monastery of Duke William of Normandy – Anselm being elected prior of Bec.

It is known that Anselm spent much of his first ten years at Bec studying the works of St Augustine of Hippo. From his earliest years in the monastery, nothing of what he may have written has survived. However, various prayers and meditations written whilst he was prior have come down to us along with his most famous works the *Monologion* and the *Proslogion* written in 1077 and 1078 respectively.

When Herluin, the Abbot and founder of Bec, died in 1078, Anselm was elected Abbot in his place. As Abbot he kept in close contact with Lanfranc, who had become Archbishop of Canterbury in 1070, following William of Normandy's triumphant invasion of England in 1066. After Lanfranc's death in 1089, the see of Canterbury was kept vacant for the following years while the king, William Rufus, enjoyed the use of the See's revenues. Because of Lanfranc's connections with Bec, Anselm was known in England. Indeed, he is known to have visited the country at least once in 1079 to inspect lands belonging to Bec. His name had been suggested by leading nobles for the appointment as Archbishop of Canterbury. The King, though, did not agree to appoint anyone, until he was suddenly struck by a serious illness that inspired him to promise to rule his kingdom more justly, and to nominate Anselm as Archbishop of Canterbury.

As Archbishop, Anselm showed himself zealous in defending the rights of the Church against the interference of the king. This stance was to lead him into exile twice, once because he insisted on travelling to Rome to discuss the reform of the English Church with the Pope, against the wishes of King William; and a second time because he refused to do homage to William's successor, King Henry I, for holding the office of Archbishop of Canterbury. A compromise was reached, however, in which the king conceded to many of Anselm's demands for the autonomy of the Church, and Anselm returned to England in 1107. Two years later, as dawn was breaking on 21st April, Anselm was called to his heavenly reward. It was Holy Week and the holy bishop died just as the monk reading him the Gospel of the day reached the words, 'You are the men who have stood by me faithfully in my trials; and now I confer a kingdom on you, just as my Father conferred one on me: you will eat and drink at my table in my kingdom.'

Anselm lived his life according to the Benedictine ideal of peace. Yet he was ever ready to risk his life for the well-being of the Church. He was never officially canonised by the Church, but was declared a Doctor of the Church in 1720, in recognition of his writings which were a humble lifelong search for a greater understanding of God.

GS

Places to visit: One can visit his birthplace at Aosta in northern Italy. Canterbury still bears something of his memory.

Further reading:

The Prayers and Meditations of St Anselm, Penguin Classics, 1973.

Church, R. W., *Life of Saint Anselm*, Macmillan, 1885.

Southern, R. W., *The Life of St Anselm, Archbishop of Canterbury, by Eadmer*, Oxford, 1972.

Southern, R. W., *Saint Anselm: A Portrait in a Landscape*, Cambridge University Press, 1991.

Southern, R. W.; Schmitt, F. S. [eds.], *Memorials of St Anselm*, Oxford University Press, 1969.

April 23rd
Solemnity

St George

HELP us fight the powers
of darkness,
Drive their legions from our coasts;
Teach us how to win the glory
Of the Almighty Lord of Hosts.

– From a popular English hymn to St George

REMEMBERED ON PUB SIGNS, flags, ships and in patriotic songs, St George is perhaps the most familiar of saints for the English, and yet among the least known. Patron of England since the 1340s, he has been almost forgotten as an early Christian martyr and is remembered more as a national symbol and the subject of romantic and knightly fables. Who was the real St George, and how did he become associated with England, damsels-in-distress, and a dragon?

Historically, we know very little about St George. In the *De Libris Recipiendis* of 496, attributed to Pope St Gelasius I, he is listed as one of the saints 'whose names are rightly reverenced among us, but whose actions are known only to God'. His story is based on two sources, one Greek, the other Latin, which both agree on the basic facts of his life. Hailing from late third-century Cappadocia, he served with distinction in the Roman army, rising to the Imperial Guard, before declaring himself a Christian in the presence of the Emperor and being sentenced to death. There followed a long and grisly series of tortures which failed to kill him – he was crushed with stones, bound to a wheel, thrown into a pit of quicklime, made to wear red-hot iron shoes, boiled in molten lead, scourged, and given poison. Finally he was decapitated – and this time, it worked. He suffered at Lydda in Palestine, around the year 303.

His cult soon spread throughout the East, as can be seen in the many church dedications, and had reached Rome by the fifth century. He was known in England from the seventh century, and appeared in Bede's Martyrology as well as on a stained-glass window at his monastery of Jarrow. However, it was with the crusades that St George became more widely known. At the Siege of Antioch in 1098, the three military saints, St George, St Mercurius and St Demetrius, appeared to the Latin troops on white horses and led them to victory. In 1191–2, Richard I visited the martyr's tomb and placed his army under his protection. It is hardly surprising that the crusaders brought back with them their veneration of the saint. Some have suggested that St George appealed to those who bemoaned the Norman invasion and looked back to a golden Anglo-Saxon age, since St George (or Georg) sounded like *geogeara* ('bygone days') and his story was similar to those of traditional English heroes, such as dragon-slaying Beowulf.

Whatever the reasons for his popularity, Archbishop Chichele of Canterbury raised the feast of St George to a *festum duplex* in 1415, to be celebrated with all the solemnity of Christmas Day itself. When Henry VIII pruned the saints' calendar in 1536, he only allowed the memorials of New Testament saints and St George to remain. However, he discouraged the traditional 'ridings' – parades with a model dragon and with actors taking on the roles of the key characters of the legend. By this time, St George had become an honorary Englishman. Born at Coventry rather than Cappadocia, the son of one Lord Albert, he killed a dragon at a location variously given, according to taste, as Dunsmore Heath (Warwickshire), Brinsop (Herefordshire), Uffington (Berkshire) or the village of St George (Derbyshire). He is also said to have fathered Guy of Warwick, another hero whose speciality was killing dragons.

What about the dragon? This seems to have been a much later addition to the story, popularised by the *Legenda Aurea* (Golden Legend) of 1265, and finding precedent in the hundred or more saints connected with dragons – including St Margaret of Antioch, eaten by a dragon which was then burst open by her making a sign of the cross, and St Carantoc, who tied one up with his stole. Moreover, dragons were widely believed to exist until early modern times, and were seen as no more exotic or fabulous than a giraffe, zebra or elephant. The story goes that a dragon terrorised part of Libya with its poisonous breath, but was appeased with sacrificial offerings, first of sheep and then of humans, chosen by lot. One day it was the turn of the king's beautiful daughter. However, St George appeared on the scene, lanced the dragon, which was then led to the city with the princess' girdle, where the beast was killed and 15,000 people were baptised. Some versions have St George marrying the princess before eventually facing a grisly martyrdom. It is not surprising that such a knightly story became the inspiration for soldiers, equestrians and orders of knighthood. The Order of the Garter, for example, founded by Edward III in 1348, had St George as patron and a magnificent chapel at Windsor as its base. The idea of 'the garter' probably came from the princess' girdle.

However, the dragon story has much Christian symbolism. The dragon is an allegory for the powers of darkness – whether it be paganism, heresy, the Christian persecutions under Diocletian (nicknamed 'the dragon') or the Devil himself. The saint, through his strong faith and his martyr's crown, thus truly defeats the metaphorical dragon. It is also interesting that St George's feast fell at the time of the Rogationtide processions for fine weather, which often involved images of dragons, the ancient symbol of winter.

St George is one of the most widely venerated of saints. The Orthodox tradition calls him the 'Great Martyr [*megalomartyros*], Athlete and Captain of the Noble Army of Martyrs'. He is a patron of many regions, including Georgia, Lithuania, Germany, Greece and (until the eighteenth century) Portugal, as well as of diverse groups, including soldiers, scouts and lepers. He is also venerated by the followers of Mohammed, most notably in the mosque of El-Khadir (= George) in Beirut.

Yet, in the end, our heavenly patron is an enigma. Mgr Ronald Knox once wrote that 'it is a peculiarity of the English that they do most things in a vague, haphazard, untidy sort of way, without being able to give any particular reasons for doing it' and that 'nothing is more characteristic of them than their choice of a patron saint'. Knox thought that he came into his own in the slogan 'St George for merry England!' Of course, 'merry England' means more than 'hearty good-fellowship' or 'beef-eating and beer-drinking jollity', for 'a country cannot be merry while it forgets God . . . a man will never be light-hearted in this world unless he is thinking of the next world; this world is too chequered an affair for that'. Let that be our prayer on the Solemnity of St George – that through the intercession of St George, all those in this country dedicated to his honour will be brought to their true homeland that is Heaven, where we will be merry for eternity.

NJS

Note: In England, to make way for the Solemnity of St George, the optional memorial of St Adalbert, formerly celebrated on 23rd April, has been moved to 24th April. This takes precedence over the other optional memorial on the general calendar of that day, St Fidelis of Sigmaringen.

Places to Visit: The church of San Giorgio in Velabro in Rome, where his relics reside, is the most significant shrine. Incidentally, this has been the titular church of many English cardinals, including that of John Henry Newman.

Further reading:

Cooney, A., *Saint George, Knight of Lydda* (an historical novel), Oxford, Family Publications, 2004

Elder, I. H., *George of Lydda. Soldier, Saint and Martyr*, London, Covenant Publishing Co., 1949.

Elvins OFM Cap, M., *St George – Who Was He?*, Ascot, Catholic Publishing Co., Ltd., undated.

Fox , D. S., *Saint George: A Saint with Three Faces*, 1983.

Marcus, G. J., *Saint George of England*, 1939.

April 29th
Feast

ST CATHERINE OF SIENA

CHARITY is the sweet and holy bond which links the soul with its Creator: it binds God with man and man with God.

– From the *Dialogues* of St Catherine of Siena

ST CATHERINE IS GIVEN a particular prominence in the new English calendar as a Patroness of Europe. She emphasises the need for the spiritual unity of the Christian nations of the continent around the See of Peter in Rome. This very concern was to take up a considerable part of her days on this earth.

She was born on the Feast of the Annunciation, 1347, into a large middle-class family of Siena. Her home, which still survives today, thanks to the devotion of the Sienese, was the focus for her early religious and mystical life. From as early as six years old, Catherine recalled distinctively mystical experiences. As a child she was known to say a Hail Mary on every step as she climbed the stairs. She was determined to live a consecrated life from before the age of twelve, although her family, wanting her to marry, resented this. Catherine was so determined that she cut off all her golden brown hair to make herself less attractive. The struggle continued for a few years and she was made to work very hard to distract her mind from religion. Eventually, finding her resolve unshaken, her family gave in.

At the age of 16 she became a third-order Dominican, and, while living at home, followed a life of intense prayer and solitude. In her longing for union with God she denied herself the pleasures of outside company. During the celebrations of Shrove Tuesday 1366, while remaining steadfast in prayer, she received the foremost experience of her life, the Mystical Marriage to Christ. To have reached the heights of the spiritual life at the tender age of nineteen is extremely rare. She was told that it was now fitting to work in the world again. She henceforth devoted herself to charitable works. Owing to her outstanding holiness she inadvertently attracted great attention and a group of followers, whom she put to good use. This informal college of the devout was aptly called by observers 'the Caterinati', and they themselves called Catherine 'Mamma'.

With notoriety also came resentment and suspicion. As a figure of growing prominence, she entered into various controversies. Some charged her of overstepping her status. She was soon called to Florence to answer charges before an ecclesiastical court. She was cleared, yet required to submit herself to a new spiritual director; this was to be Bl. Raymond of Capua. He was to become her closest friend and confidant, and to write the first biography of her after her death. Catherine soon won over her enemies and became evermore involved in politics and arbitrations in the city.

In February 1375, Catherine received another intense mystical experience of the crucified Christ and she was given the gift and the trial of bearing the Holy Stigmata on her own body. This event coincides with her call to enter into the world politics of her day, which provided for her immense sufferings and would ultimately cut short her fragile life. In her promotion of a new Crusade to rescue the Holy Places, Catherine had come to know Gregory XI, and she would write often to him as 'my sweet Babbo'. The unity of Christendom was seriously under threat, with the Vicar of Christ living in Avignon, far away from Rome. There was also an anti-papal religious rebellion in several Italian states, and France was under interdict. In her petitions for peace and unity she came into contact with many of the great rulers of her day. In 1376, owing to her renown, Catherine was called to represent

Florence as an ambassador to Gregory XI. On arrival at Avignon, Catherine went straight to the point: 'Return to Rome!' She had come to know by divine means a secret vow he had made to return, so she said to him 'Fulfil what you have promised'. On 13th September 1376, Pope Gregory returned to Rome, ending nearly seventy years of absence.

Catherine returned to Florence where she eventually established peace with the Holy See. On returning to her beloved Siena, she began to work on a summary of her spiritual teaching, *The Dialogues*. This was to become one of the great classics of Christian literature. Along with around four hundred letters, this constitutes her literary output. For its profound and enlightening content, she was named Doctor of the Church in 1970. This is even more remarkable considering that she was formally illiterate. She had never learned to write and had received no formal education. Her understanding and capacity had come by means of an infused grace.

Only two years after the end of the 'Babylonian Captivity' of the Papacy in Avignon, there began the 'Great Schism' which would last forty years. Gregory XI had died in 1378, and while Urban VI was elected successor in Rome, an anti-pope was set up in Avignon. Catherine wore herself out in trying to gain support for Urban. She journeyed to Rome to support the beleaguered Pope. She became very close to him, and firmly led him to modify his natural harshness of character. After suffering a stroke in early 1380, she died in April of that year in Rome. She had declared on her deathbed, 'Hold firm to this, my beloved, that I have given my life for the holy Church'.

She was immediately acclaimed by the people as a saint and the spontaneous cult was confirmed in 1461 when she was canonised by the Church. She was a great reformer whose efforts for a Christendom united around one Pope in Rome would be finally realised many years after her death. In a difficult age she issued a call to purification and repentance which alone could save Christian and European unity. Her common emblem is, fittingly, the lily.

On 1st October 1999, when St Catherine was declared patroness of Europe, John Paul II wrote 'Thus may Europe grow! May it grow as a Europe of the spirit, in continuity with the best of its history, of which holiness is the highest expression'.

MPH

Places to visit: In Siena her house is preserved as a shrine, as is an early portrait and the relic of her head in San Domenico. She is buried in Rome, near Blessed Fra Angelico, in Santa Maria sopra Minerva, the titular Church of Cardinal Cormac Murphy O'Connor.

Further Reading:

Antony, C. M., *Saint Catherine of Siena: Her Life and Times*, London, Burns & Oates, 1916.

de la Bedoyère, M., *Catherine, Saint of Siena*, Hollis & Carter, 1947.

Curtayne, A., *Saint Catherine of Siena*, London, Sheed and Ward, 1929.

Gillet, M. S., *The Mission of St Catherine*, St Louis, B. Herder Book Co., 1955.

Thorold, A. (ed.), *The Dialogue of Saint Catherine of Siena*, Rockford, TAN Books, 1974.

de Wohl, L., *Lay Siege to Heaven: A Novel of Saint Catherine of Siena*, New York, J. B Lippincott Company, 1960. Republished by Ignatius Press, San Francisco, undated.

May 4th
Memorial

The English Martyrs

CAN we religiously suppose that the blood of our Martyrs, three centuries ago and since, shall never receive its recompense? ... The long barbarous sentence, the savage execution, the rack, the gibbet, the knife, the cauldron, the numberless tortures of those holy victims, O my God, are they to have no reward?
... And in the day of trial and desolation for England, when hearts were pierced through and through with Mary's woe, at the crucifixion of Thy body mystical, was not every tear that flowed, and every drop of blood that was shed, the seeds of a future harvest, when they who sowed in sorrow were to reap in joy?

– John Henry Newman,
The Second Spring

IN THE SIXTEENTH AND SEVENTEENTH CENTURIES, over a period of 150 years, several hundred men and women, from all walks of life and social backgrounds, gave their lives for the Catholic faith in England and Wales. The majority were hanged, drawn and quartered, a few were beheaded, and some died after a long imprisonment or under torture. Of these, over 300 are recognised by the Church as Saint or Blessed. One cannot over-estimate their influence on the religious consciousness of English

Catholics during the last two centuries. English Catholicism could have disappeared completely during the reformation period as it had done in many northern European states, yet these martyrs lived and died to preserve it. The particular reasons for martyrdom were many and varied, yet always for motives of faith, with one over-riding and ever-present issue, the upholding of the Pope in his authority as Supreme Pastor of the Universal Church.

The first martyr was a Carthusian prior, St John Houghton, executed for refusing to acknowledge the Act of Supremacy soon after Henry VIII's break with Rome in 1535 (the same year that Sts Thomas More and John Fisher gave up their lives). After Henry's reign there are no recognised martyrs until the Northern Rising of 1569 against the government, and Elizabeth's excommunication by Pius V in 1570, after which the persecution of Catholics increased in extent and intensity. However, the period of persecution was by no means consistent: often, there would be years of relative peace and co-existence, then a sudden burst of prosecutions, imprisonments and executions in the aftermath of some diplomatic 'scare' or a discovered 'plot', such as the Spanish Armada of 1588, the Gunpowder plot of 1605, or the Titus Oates controversy in 1678. Many of the martyrs came from Elizabeth's long reign, including some particularly famous names: Cuthbert Mayne, Edmund Campion, Ralph Sherwin, Robert Southwell, and Henry Walpole. During this period various foreign seminaries were founded to train English Catholic priests, most notably at Douai in Flanders, Valladolid in Spain, and the Venerable English College in Rome from which 44 men died for the faith. The last of the recognised English martyrs is William Viscount Stafford, beheaded in 1680 for alleged treason (Oliver Plunkett, Irish Bishop of Armagh, being treated separately). Persecutions still did not cease for over a century, yet the most furious storm had passed and the survival of Catholicism in England had been assured.

Every part of the country has a connection with the martyrs and their shrines are numerous. From the Tyburns of London and York to the grand recusant houses with their priest holes and hidden altars, the martyrs are venerated and remembered. The seminaries are still imbued with the spirit of the martyrs. The English Colleges in Rome and Valladolid, founded in the late 16th century during the height of the persecutions, still exist on their original sites, training students to continue the work of the missionary priests. A vast number of parishes and schools are dedicated to them and possess their sacred relics and images. The one and only complete relic of an English martyr lies in Westminster Cathedral. St John Southworth, a Lancastrian who was particularly devoted to the poor of London's streets, is honoured there in the chapel of St George and the English Martyrs.

There have been various beatifications and canonisations of the English martyrs between 1886 and 1987. On 25th October 1970, Pope Paul VI canonised 40 of the English Martyrs. He wrote, 'they will assist in advancing an ecumenism worthy of the name. They will be a true safeguard to those real values in which the genuine peace and prosperity of human society are rooted.' They continue to be powerful intercessors for the faithful and their memory still inspires a love of the Church and the Pope, of the Priesthood and the Mass.

MPH

List of the 40 Martyrs of England and Wales canonised in 1970 by Pope Paul VI

John Almond (5th December)
Edmund Arrowsmith (28th August)
Ambrose Barlow (11th September)
John Boste (24th July)
Alexander Bryant (1st December)
Edmund Campion (1st December)
Margaret Clitherow (21st October)
Philip Evans (22nd July)
Thomas Garnet (26th June)
Edmund Gennings (10th December)
Richard Gwyn (17th October)
John Houghton (4th May)
Philip Howard (19th October)
John Jones (12th July)
John Kemble (22nd August)
Luke Kirby (30th May)
Robert Lawrence (4th May)
David Lewis (27th August)
Anne Line (27th February)
John Lloyd (22nd July)
Cuthbert Mayne (29th November)
Henry Morse (1st February)
Nicholas Owen (2nd March)
John Payne (2nd April)
Polydore Plasden (10th December)
John Plessington (19th July)
Richard Reynolds (4th May)
John Rigby (19th June)
John Roberts (9th December)
Alban Roe (21st January)
Ralph Sherwin (1st December)
Robert Southwell (21st February)
John Southworth (27th June)
John Stone (12th May)
John Wall (22nd August)
Henry Walpole (7th April)
Margaret Ward (30th August)
Augustine Webster (4th May)
Swithun Wells (10th December)
Eustace White (10th December)

Places to visit: The shrines connected to the martyrs of England and Wales are many and varied: the two remaining foreign seminaries in Rome and Valladolid, where many of the martyr priests trained, preserve the very rooms where they lived and a substantial number of relics and images; Tyburn Convent in London, the place of execution for so many of the martyrs, is a site of pilgrimage run by Benedictine sisters; there is a Marian shrine and recusant house with many relics and a missionary recusant altar at Ladyewell, near Preston in Lancashire; there is also a large number of recusant family homes with hiding holes, for instance at Harvington Hall near Worcester and Stonor Park near Henley-on-Thames, where missionary priests would conceal themselves from the authorities.

Further Reading:

The Martyrs of England and Wales 1535 to 1680 – a Chronological List, CTS, 1967.

Bowden, H., *Mementoes of the English Martyrs*, London, 1910.

Caraman, P. (collected and edited), *The Other Face: Catholic Life Under Elizabeth I*, Sheed and Ward, 1960.

Challoner, R., *Martyrs to the Catholic Faith in England 1577–1684* (many editions).

Waugh, E., *Edmund Campion*, 1934 (many editions).

Whinder, R. (ed.), *The Forty-Four: The Martyrs of the Venerable English College*, Farnborough, St Michael's Abbey Press, 1999.

May 19th
Optional Memorial

St Dunstan

O King of Nations and their desire; the Cornerstone, who makest both one: Come and save mankind, whom thou formedst of clay.

– From St Dunstan's hymn *O Rex Gentium*

ST DUNSTAN WAS BORN at Glastonbury, the nephew of Athelmus, Archbishop of Canterbury. It was the year 924, ten years after the death of Alfred the Great, a time when England was suffering greatly as a result of the incursions of the Danes. For a time it seemed as if Dunstan himself might be directly involved in such political affairs, for as a young man his uncle's influence obtained a place for him in the court of King Athelstan. His family no doubt hoped that he would obtain a position of power and influence, but Dunstan soon decided that a courtier's life was not for him, and chose to become a priest instead.

He lived at the abbey of Glastonbury as a sort of hermit, spending his time in a workshop where he created crosses, thuribles and sacred vessels, as well as vestments for the liturgy, and he copied and illuminated books. We know that Dunstan played the harp and loved to sing. But Dunstan was not to remain for long in his retreat. The unsettled state of England needed good men to take a more prominent part in public life, and Dunstan heeded the call. In the year 939 King Athelstan died, and his successor Edmund, who knew and admired Dunstan, had him appointed as the nineteenth Abbot of Glastonbury. When Edmund was murdered in 946, his uncle Edred ruled in his place, and Dunstan became his close advisor, remaining so for many years, until in 955 King Edred died and was replaced by Edmund's son Edwi.

Edwi had very little time for Abbot Dunstan's advice and lived an openly immoral lifestyle, even leaving his coronation banquet to go and visit a concubine. When Dunstan denounced Edwi's way of life, the king promptly sent him into exile, and Dunstan remained abroad for a year. By the end of that time, Edwi had already become unpopular. Mercia and the northern provinces of his kingdom rejected his leadership and crowned his brother Edgar in his place. Dunstan returned to England and was made Bishop of Worcester. Soon afterwards he became Bishop of London simultaneously, a highly unusual situation, but justified by the disorder of the times and the complete lack of suitable candidates for the episcopacy.

Edwi died in 959 and Edgar became the sole King of England. He quickly moved to appoint Dunstan as Archbishop of Canterbury, in addition to which Pope John XII appointed him as a papal legate. Armed with this authority, Dunstan set about the much-needed work of reform. He was assisted in this by St Ethelwold of Winchester and St Oswald of York, two other zealous bishops of the time. One object of this reform was to remove clergy who had abandoned their lives of celibacy. At Winchester Dunstan removed the whole chapter of secular canons and replaced them with monks for this reason. He demanded high moral standards of the laity too, even the most powerful. When King Edgar seduced a girl who had been placed under the protection of the nuns of Wilton Abbey, Dunstan rebuked his sin with such fervour that Edgar was moved to repentance. He undertook a seven-year penance in reparation, during which time he was not allowed to wear his crown, had to fast twice a week, and was obliged to give considerable sums to the poor.

Edgar died in 975 and was succeeded by his son Edward, 'the martyr', who was murdered after a short reign, and was followed by his brother Ethelred. Ethelred was crowned by Dunstan himself in 979, but the saint predicted that he would have a disastrous reign, which sadly came to pass. From this time on, Dunstan seems to have had little influence on public affairs. He retired to his own cathedral city, and spent his time in the management of his diocese, prayer and study. He was known to have a particular devotion to the saints of Canterbury, visiting their tombs by night to spend long hours in prayer.

Finally the time came for St Dunstan to be removed from this world, and to discover the peace he had sought for long ago in his little hermitage at Glastonbury. He died at Canterbury on 27th May 988, the Saturday after the Ascension, and was buried in the Cathedral.

RW

Places to visit: The ruins of Glastonbury abbey; Canterbury Cathedral where he was first laid to rest beneath the choir.

Further Reading:

Dales, D., *Dunstan: Saint and Statesman*, 1988.

Duckett, E. S., *St Dunstan of Canterbury*, London, Collins, 1955.

Knowles OSB, D., *The Monastic Order in England from the Times of St Dunstan to the Fourth Lateran Council 940–1216*, Cambridge University Press, 1966.

Rambeys (ed.), *St Dunstan: His Life, Times and Cult*, Boydell, 1992.

Robinson, J. A., *The Times of Saint Dunstan*, Oxford, Clarendon Press, 1923.

May 25th
Memorial

St Bede the Venerable

VENERABILIS BEDA PRESBITER ET MONCHVS ORD S. Benedicti. May. 27. Mart. baes. f.

I PRAY you, noble Jesus, that as you have graciously granted me joyfully to imbibe the words of your knowledge, so You will also of your bounty grant me to come at length to yourself, the Fount of all wisdom, and to dwell in your presence for ever.

– St Bede at the end of his *Ecclesiastical History*

PERHAPS THE BEST KNOWN of all the English saints, Bede the Venerable is a Doctor of the Church and the father of English history. To him we owe much of our knowledge of early Christianity in these isles. As the last of the great Fathers of the western Church, his works were a formative part of the intellectual edifice of medieval Christendom and are indeed still used today in the divine office of the Church. His influence in the West ranks alongside that of St Gregory the Great and St Anselm.

He was born in 673 and grew up near the monastery of Wearmouth. As early as the age of seven he was sent to the monastery for education under the tutelage of the holy Benet Biscop. Later he moved to the new monastery of Jarrow and came under the influence of another saint, Ceolfrith. Between Wearmouth and Jarrow he would spend virtually all his days. He was ordained deacon at 18 and priest at 29.

Few comparably great figures of history have been so stationary and little travelled. Near the end of his life he would say, 'I have devoted my energies to the study of the Scriptures, observing monastic discipline, and singing the daily services in church; study, teaching and writing have always been my delight.' We hear of only two journeys outside the monastery. Once to Lindisfarne to research the life of St Cuthbert, and once to Archbishop Egbert in York to whom he offered guidance and direction. Yet, for one so little travelled, he showed remarkable knowledge of the geography, history and political situation of his country.

He considered his twenty-five richly allegorical scripture commentaries as his greatest works. In these he displayed knowledge of Latin, Greek and a little Hebrew, as well as a deep immersion in the tradition of the Fathers. He also wrote influential works on practical and empirical matters such as the calendar and explanations of natural phenomena. He wrote some works in the vernacular which are now lost, yet is considered one of the fathers of English prose. He wrote the original Latin of the hymns 'The hymn for conquering martyrs raise' and 'Sing we triumphant hymns of praise'.

It is his collection of historical works that is most celebrated today. He wrote two important lives of St Cuthbert and a short history of the Abbots of Wearmouth and Jarrow. The most important of all was *The Ecclesiastical History of the English People* completed in 731. This is one of the most important historical / hagiographical accounts of the first millennium A.D. (incidentally, it was Bede who popularised the use of 'Anno Domini'). While maintaining a remarkable sobriety of judgment and balanced objectivity throughout, it unashamedly and openly adds a theological interpretation to history. He sought to trace the story of how the English peoples had been 'called out of darkness into God's wonderful light'. Fascinated by the characters in this historical drama, Bede gave us a huge amount of precious information about the great figures and characters of the age: Augustine, Paulinus, Edwin, Oswald, Aidan, and so many others. Cardinal William Allen in the 16th century used to encourage his recusant seminarians to read Bede's history to get a true sense of their tradition and a conviction of the apostolic continuity of English Catholicism.

He was working on a vernacular translation of the Gospel of St John up until his last day. We possess a moving account of his death from one of his monks named Cuthbert. After distributing from his desk some peppercorns, napkins and incense, the meagre possessions he had in this world, he said to his brothers, 'It is time that I return to Him who formed me. I have lived long: the time of my dissolution draws nigh, and I desire to be dissolved and be with Christ'. When evening came, the boy who was writing down the translation said, 'Dear master, there is yet one sentence to be written'. After Bede had finished his dictation, the boy said, 'The sentence is finished now', to which Bede responded, 'Thou hast well said, it is finished! . . . Raise my head in thy hands; for I wish to be facing the holy place where I was wont to pray, and as I lie to call upon my Father'. He passed away at the Trinitarian invocation while singing the vespers of the Ascension. It was 27th May 735.

Writing of Bede's death, the great apostle St Boniface wrote, 'The candle of the Church, lit by the Holy Spirit, was extinguished'. Bede was born into a missionary land, he died in a country with a mission, a great mission to the Germanic peoples of Europe, which he had greatly influenced and would continue to inspire.

His cult was well established very soon after his death. Alcuin records that miracles followed the veneration of his relics, which were dispersed as far as Fulda in Germany. In the 11th century, his relics were translated from Jarrow to Durham. Indeed it is possible that his relics still rest in the Galilee Chapel of Durham Cathedral, having survived the ravages of the Reformation.

MPH

Places to visit: The monastic ruins of Jarrow and Wearmouth where St Bede spent his whole monastic life.

Further Reading:

Bede, *The Ecclesiastical History of the English People* (many editions).

Davidson, H. E., *The Golden Age of Northumbria*, Longmans, 1960.

Gillett, H. M., *St Bede the Venerable*, Burns, Oates & Washbourne, 1935.

Hume, B., *Footprints of the Northern Saints*, DLT, 1996.

Marsden, J.; Gregory, J. (translator), *The Illustrated Bede*, Edinburgh, Floris Books, 1996.

Mayr-Harting, H., *The Coming of Christianity to Anglo-Saxon England*, Penn State Press, 1972.

May 27th
Memorial

St Augustine

WE PRAY thee, O Lord, in all thy mercy, that thy wrath and anger may be turned away from this city and from thy holy house, for we are sinners. Alleluia.

– Prayer sung by St Augustine and his monks as they approached Canterbury

SINCE THE 1400TH ANNIVERSARY in 1997 of his arriving, there has been a renewal of interest in the 'Apostle of England'. Landing on the shores of Kent at the end of the 6th century, St Augustine's mission marked a significant moment in the history of the English peoples.

Augustine had been a Roman monk in the monastery of St Andrew on the Caelian Hill, founded by Gregory the Great. In this centre of religious life he received his training and was caught up in the same apostolic fervour as his teacher and master, Gregory. Circumstances in England had opened up an unprecedented opportunity for evangelisation, and Gregory was eager to release monks for apostolic purposes, just as he had left the security of the cloister for a ministry as successor of St Peter.

In the year 596, Augustine set out with a small band of monks from Rome for the island of Britannia. En route they passed through the Gaulish

Kingdoms of France. It was here that doubts set in about the possibilities of the success of a mission to such a barbarous people. It was only Gregory's exhortation to trust and to bravery that convinced Augustine and his men to continue undaunted.

The small band of men arrived at Ebbsfleet in 597. They were met by a royal entourage. King Ethelbert of Kent, overlord of all the southern English, met them in the open air, superstitious and fearful of what they might bring. The Monks processed, singing a solemn litany, bearing a silver cross and carrying an icon of Christ. There was no spectacular immediate conversion, but the King was friendly and impressed and allowed them to establish a dwelling and to practise their religion. They established themselves in a common life outside the city walls of Canterbury, around an old Romano-British church dedicated to St Martin, where Ethelbert's wife Bertha, a Gaulish Christian, was known to worship. They soon built a monastery nearby, which would later become the burial place of the Saints, Archbishops and Kings of Canterbury, one of the greatest shrines in England. They attracted the native people by their goodness, their preaching and miracles.

Before long, owing much to the influence of Bertha, his Gaulish Christian wife, the great miracles of Augustine, and the political motivations of becoming closer to the continent (especially Gaul), Ethelbert himself embraced the faith of Christ and became the first English Christian king. A flood of catechumens now followed Ethelbert into the waters of baptism. Bede tells us that on Christmas Day 597 at least 10,000 were born anew in the Holy Spirit.

Augustine kept a continual written contact with Gregory, informing him of the mission's success and asking advice on countless issues. Before long the Pope granted approval for him to establish a permanent Church in this land and to be consecrated as first bishop, father of the English hierarchy, succeeding from the apostles. Augustine travelled to Arles in Gaul for his consecration at the hands of Archbishop Etherius. In 601 the Pope despatched to him the Pallium, the symbol of Primatial authority.

King Ethelbert gave them a great palace of his in Canterbury. Near to this Augustine began to build a cathedral church using Roman foundations. He named it Christ Church. Upon this the present Cathedral stands as a great shrine and testimony to the conversion of the nation. It was here that Augustine set up his Metropolitan See, rather than in the ancient Roman city of London as Pope Gregory had expected. This shows how carefully and prudently Augustine worked with King Ethelbert, always respecting his temporal authority and knowing the conversion of the people was dependent upon his support. Rather than eradicating the many neutral elements of the native paganism, such as the local festivals and temples, he managed to incorporate them into authentic Christian life and worship. He also helped the King draft, as far as we know, the first written laws of the English people.

Although his policy was primarily one of consolidation and establishment in one area, he founded the two dioceses of Rochester and London (the town of the East Saxons) which were under Ethelbert's control. He tried to establish a proper ecclesial relationship with the ancient 'Celtic' church to the west (particularly in Wales). At a place near the Bristol channel, posthumously called 'Augustine's Oak', Augustine exhorted the leaders of the 'Celtic' church to accept a greater unity with established Roman customs (particularly over the date of Easter) and with his mission to the English peoples. Despite his best efforts and even his healing of a blind man to prove that God was with him, Augustine failed to convince them. He made a prophecy, warning that they would suffer and continue to decline so long as they refused Christian fellowship. Bede comments 'By divine judgement, all these things happened as Augustine foretold'.

Augustine died on 26th May, 604, and was buried near the unfinished Church of Sts Peter and Paul (the monastery he had founded). His body was later moved into the Church by his successor, Archbishop Laurentius, with an inscription attesting to his great and apostolic achievements. Devotion to Augustine through the ages has been considerable, and the account of his missionary journey told by the Venerable Bede has helped shape the religious identity of the English Church through the centuries.

MPH

Places to Visit: The world heritage site of St Augustine's Abbey in Canterbury, along with the Cathedral and the ancient church of St Martin.

Further Reading:

Deanesley, M., *St Augustine of Canterbury*, St Austin Press, 1997.

Gameson, R. (ed), *St Augustine and the conversion of England*, Sutton, 1999.

Gasquet OSB, A. Cardinal, *The Mission of St Augustine and other addresses*, London, G. Bell & Sons, 1924.

Hunter Blair, P., *The World of Bede*, New York, St Martin's Press, 1970.

Marett-Crosby OSB, A., *Foundations of Christian England: Augustine of Canterbury and His Impact*, Ampleforth Abbey, 1997.

Mayr-Harting, H., *The Coming of Christianity to Anglo-Saxon England*, Penn State Press, 1972.

June 5th
Memorial

ST BONIFACE

LET us not be dumb dogs, sleeping sentinels, hired men that fly at the sight of the wolf: but watchful and diligent pastors, preaching to the great and the small, to the rich and the poor, to every age and condition, being constant in season and out of season.

– St Boniface, Epistle IX

ST BONIFACE, who was without doubt one of the greatest missionaries of all time, discovered his vocation very early in life. He was born at Crediton, Devon. As a child he encountered some wandering monks who were preaching the gospel in the west of England, and who came to stay at his father's house in Crediton. Boniface (whose baptismal name was Winfrid) decided that he would chose the same way of life as them. He entered the abbey of Nutcell, and here he studied and became a teacher, although he was not actually ordained a priest until the age of thirty.

A few years after his ordination, his life underwent a change. Unwavering in his commitment to Christ, Winfrid realised he was being called to leave the quiet life of the cloisters and undertake missionary work instead. He set off on his first mission in the year 716. There were, however, initial difficulties. His first mission was to Frisia, or Friesland (modern-day

Netherlands), where there were already English missionaries working, but things had recently taken a turn for the worse. Radbod, a new ruler, who was violently anti-Christian, was making missionary work impossible. Boniface found no alternative but an immediate return to England. Here a new difficulty emerged. His community elected him abbot, which would have made missionary work impossible. Fortunately, Bishop Daniel of Winchester was able to release Winfrid from this unwelcome office and encouraged him in his dedication to the missions.

In 719, armed with letters of introduction from Daniel, Winfrid travelled to Rome to see Pope Gregory II and obtain his blessing as a missionary. The pope gave it willingly, as well as many relics to be used in the building of new churches. Armed with this encouragement, Winfrid returned to Germany. He travelled through Bavaria and Thuringia, baptising pagans and reforming the lives of the Christians he found there. At this time, Duke Radbod died, and Charles Martel, Mayor of the Place de France and a great friend to Christianity, ruled in his place. Winfrid therefore hastened to Frisia and helped St Willibrord in his work there. He was so zealous that Willibrord wanted Winfrid to succeed him as Archbishop of Utrecht, but Winfrid no more desired to be a bishop than he had wanted to be made abbot, and he persuaded Willibrord to let him go.

Leaving Frisia, he set off to preach the faith in Hesse and Saxony. Wherever he went he made huge numbers of converts, and this came to the ears of Pope Gregory II, who summoned him to Rome and declared his intention of making Winfrid a bishop. Since the order came from the Pope himself, Boniface could no longer refuse the honour. He was made a bishop, and at the same time made a special promise of loyalty to the successors of Peter. On this visit the Pope confirmed the new name which, it appears, Winfrid had already been using for some time, and from now on he was universally known as Boniface.

Boniface's work as a missionary was incredible. Not only did he convert huge numbers, but he spared himself no physical effort in spreading the faith. At Geismar, in modern-day Germany, he personally chopped down an enormous oak tree which was being used for the worship of Wodin. (It is from this incident that the German people fancifully derive the origins of the Christmas tree). In 723 a new Pope, Gregory III, created Boniface Primate of All Germany, and sent him the Pallium from Rome. His missionary activity soon created the need for new dioceses, so in 738 Boniface visited

Rome for the third time and was made a legate of the Holy See. In this capacity he created the dioceses of Salzburg, Freisinghein, Ratisbon, Erfurt, Buraberg, Wurtzburg and Eichstatt, while he fixed his own metropolitan See at Mainz.

Despite so many achievements, Boniface was still not happy to rest on his laurels, nor to enjoy in peace the fruits of a lifetime's hard work. He had promised to serve God as a missionary, and as a missionary he intended to die. In 753 he placed his archdiocese in the hands of St Lullus and set off to preach the faith in the dangerous territory of East Friesland. Here as before, his preaching attracted converts in large numbers, but he also attracted hostility. On the eve of Pentecost, 757, as he was preparing to administer confirmation to many new Christians on the following day, Boniface and fifty-two of his companions were slaughtered by an enraged army of pagans. It is exactly the way he would have chosen to die. His body was later recovered from the site and buried with respect at Fulda, an abbey which he himself had founded, and where his shrine can be found today. Thus was laid to rest the man who, more than any other human being, was responsible for establishing the Christian faith between the Danube and the Rhine. It is perhaps not surprising that the Catholic historian Christopher Dawson referred to St Boniface as 'a man who had a greater influence on the history of Europe than any Englishman who ever lived'.

RW

Places to Visit: His tomb is still preserved and honoured at Fulda in Germany.

Further Reading:

St Boniface, *Letters of St Boniface*, Cambridge University Press, 2000.

Cox, G. W., *The Life of Saint Boniface, Archbishop of Mayence and Apostle of Germany*, London, Joseph Masters, 1853.

Kurth, G., *St Boniface*, Milwaukee, Bruce Publishing Company, 1935.

Reuter, T. (ed.), *The Greatest Englishman, Essays on St Boniface and the Church at Crediton*, Exeter, 1980.

Br. Roberto CSC, *Bring me an ax! A story of St Boniface of Germany*, Dujarie Press, 1964.

Talbot, C. H. (transl. & ed.), *The Anglo-Saxon Missionaries in Germany*, Sheed and Ward, London, 1954.

June 9th
Optional Memorial

St Columba

I COMMEND to you, my children, these last words of mine, that you keep among you unfeigned love with peace.

– From the last words of St Columba

COLUMBA (sometimes rendered as Col Cil or Colum Cille) was born in Garten in Donegal around the year 520, a son of the royal Ui Neill clan. Legend says that his birth was predicted by many earlier Irish saints. The *Life of Columba* by the monk Adomnan says that 'From his boyhood, Colum Cille devoted himself to the Christian combat and to the search for wisdom'.

As a monk he studied under the celebrated Finnian of Clonard in County Meath. Shortly after this he founded a monastery around which the city of Derry was later to rise. The saint went on to found further monasteries all over Ireland including those at Durrow (County Offaly), Kells (County Meath) and Glencolmcille (County Donegal).

In 565, Columba left Ireland with twelve companions, travelling to Iona, an island off south-west Scotland. The exact reasons for his departure have never been clear, but his decision may have been rooted in the desire for a form of mission which was often referred to as 'pilgrimage', a voluntary exile for Christ. On Iona, Adomnan tells us, Columba 'could not let even one hour pass that was not given to prayer or reading or writing or some other good work. Night and day he so unwearyingly gave himself to fasts and vigils that the burden of each single work seemed beyond the strength of man. Yet through all he was loving to everyone, his holy face was always cheerful, and in his inmost heart he was happy with the joy of the Holy Spirit.'

Adomnan, whose biography is one of the most important texts of this type from the middle ages, describes Columba as a tall man of powerful build and of scholarly skill and zealous commitment to God's work. Columba converted Brude, king of the picts; and the Irish king, Aidan of Dalriade, was consecrated by him. He founded two churches in Inverness, and his followers founded many more in the west of Scotland and the Western Isles.

His skill as a scribe may still be seen in the Cathach of Columba, a late sixth-century psalter in the Irish Academy. This skill helped sustain him as his energy waned over the last four years of his life. When he knew that death was near, he called his brothers to him, saying, 'I commend to you, my children, these last words of mine, that you keep among you unfeigned love with peace'. Just before Matins, early next morning, while blessing his monastic community, he breathed his last.

Not by chance, in the same year that Columba died (597), a new band of missionaries, this time from the south, was arriving in Kent to begin its work of evangelisation. In a symmetry, worthy only of divine providence, St Augustine takes over where St Columba left off, proclaiming, albeit in different ways, the one Faith of Christ. As the Ionian missionary influence would continue from the north, the influence of the Roman missionaries would advance from the south. Eventually both would combine, to fulfil that great work of the conversion of the Anglo-Saxon peoples.

Although the relics of Columba were removed from Iona to Dunkeld after the repeated Viking raids in the 9th century, the island and its monastic ruin still preserve something of his memory, a place of great holiness and pilgrimage.

GS

Places to Visit: The island of Iona, Scotland.

Further Reading:

Chadwick, N. K.; Newbigin, L.; Morton, T. R., *St Columba: Fourteenth Centenary*, Glasgow, Iona Community Publishing Department, 1963.

Colum, P., *The Legend of Saint Columba*, Sheed & Ward, 1936.

Gwynn, Denis, *St Columba*, London, Catholic Truth Society, 1934.

Hume, B., *Footprints of the Northern Saints*, DLT, 1996.

of Iona, Adomnan; Sharpe, R. (trans.), *Life of St Columba*, Penguin, 1995.

Mayr-Harting, H., *The Coming of Christianity to Anglo-Saxon England*, Penn State Press, 1972.

Menzies, L., *St Columba of Iona*, Glasgow, Iona Community, 1954.

Tranter, N., *St Columba*, London, Coronet Books, 1995.

Troup, G. E., *Saint Columba, The Lord's Song in a Strange Land*, London, T. N. Foulis, 1913.

June 16th
Optional Memorial

ST RICHARD OF CHICHESTER

THANKS be to thee, my Lord Jesus Christ, for all the benefits thou hast given me, for all the pains and insults which thou hast borne for me. O most merciful redeemer, friend and brother, may I know thee more clearly, love thee more dearly and follow thee more nearly, day by day.

– St Richard of Chichester

ST RICHARD was born in 1197, in the manor of Wiche, four miles from Worcester. As a young man he studied at Oxford, but unlike Chaucer's 'clerke of Oxenforde' Richard possessed a good practical mind as well as book-learning. When his elder brother mismanaged his estates and faced financial ruin, Richard went to work for him as a servant, and by his talent managed to restore the family fortunes. This done, he continued his studies in Paris, returned to Oxford to take a Master's degree and then went on for still further studies at the university of Bologna, eventually becoming a canon lawyer in that city. Here he came under the influence of the newly founded Order of Preachers and the famous teacher John of Vicenza. Throughout his days, Richard would turn to the Dominican Order for spiritual and intellectual guidance. His confessor and friend, Ralph Bocking, was a Black Friar to whom we owe Richard's first biography.

Returning to England, he became Chancellor of Oxford University in 1235. He had befriended some of the greatest men of his day, including Robert Grosseteste and Edmund Rich. It was Edmund, as the new Archbishop of Canterbury, who persuaded him to become Chancellor of that archdiocese. In this capacity Richard sided with St Edmund in his dispute with King Henry III over the liberty of the Church and followed his bishop into exile, in 1240, to France. Only at this stage was he ordained a priest, having only been in minor orders before. He returned to England and worked as a simple priest until Archbishop Boniface of Canterbury (St Edmund's successor) restored him to his post as Chancellor of the diocese.

In 1244 Henry III appointed his favourite, Robert Passelaw, to the vacant diocese of Chichester, but Archbishop Boniface refused to recognise the King's appointment and selected Richard as bishop instead. Henry was furious and seized all the revenues of the See. Fortunately, as we saw before, Richard was no stranger to royal fury, and refused to be intimidated. He defended his case vigorously and appealed to Pope Innocent IV at Rome. Papal support forced Henry to back down, and after two years the revenues were returned to those to whom they belonged.

Richard soon proved himself an exemplary bishop, hard-working and famous for his acts of charity. His steward is supposed to have complained on one occasion that there was no money left for further alms. 'Then sell my plate and horse', replied the saint. Once, while celebrating Holy Mass, he is said to have dropped the chalice which miraculously remained unspilled. It is for this reason that he is often depicted in Christian art with a chalice at his feet.

At the end of his life he was asked by the Pope to help in preaching a crusade, and he was doing this when he died, at Dover, on 3rd May 1253. At his own request he was buried by the altar dedicated to his greatest friend, St Edmund. His feast day was formerly kept on the anniversary of his death, but since this often falls in Lent this has now been moved to June 16th. This was the date on which his relics were transferred to a new shrine in his cathedral church of Chichester. This shrine was destroyed by Protestant reformers in the 16th century and his relics buried secretly.

RW

Places to Visit: Chichester Cathedral, the place of his original shrine

Further Reading:

Arnold, H. E. B., *St Richard of Wyche, Bishop of Chichester*, reproduced from *The Sussex County Magazine*, April 1935, Simmath Press, Roseangle, Dundee, 1935.

Duncan Jones, C. M., *St Richard of Chichester*, Faith Press, 1974.

Jacob, E. F., 'St Richard of Chichester', *Journal of Ecclesiastical History* (vii), 1956.

Jones, D., *Saint Richard of Chichester. The Sources for his Life*, Sussex Record Society, Volume 79, 1993.

Reginald Capes, M., *Richard of Wyche – Labourer, Bishop, Saint*, London, Sands.

June 20th
Optional Memorial

St Alban

IF YOU wish to know the truth about my religion, know that I am a Christian, and am bound by the laws of Christ.

– The words of St Alban at his trial, recorded in Bede's *Ecclesiastical History*

ST ALBAN, our Proto-Martyr, takes us right back to the origins of Christianity in Britain. Various legends attribute the introduction of the Faith in Britain to St Philip the Apostle, St Paul, and St Joseph of Arimathea. Modern writers posit the less colourful theory of contacts being made, perhaps through trade, with the early Christian communities in Gaul, or even the influence of resident converted Roman leaders and soldiers. If, as some scholars suggest, we can date St Alban's martyrdom to as early as 209, then it is clear that Christianity must have reached Britain within a century and a half after the Resurrection.

St Alban was a soldier in the large Roman town of Verulamium, now known as St Albans. He sheltered a fugitive priest and, impressed by his piety and example, was instructed and converted by him. When soldiers arrived to search the house, St Alban wrapped himself in the priest's cloak, and was arrested. The priest – traditionally called St Amphibalus, which means 'cloak' – thus escaped, and St Alban, refusing to offer sacrifices to the gods, was flogged and handed over to the executioners.

The passion of St Alban involved a string of miracles. As he was being escorted to Holmhurst Hill, he dried up the river to afford a crossing for himself and the crowds that followed him. One of the executioners fell at his feet and declared that he would either die with him or in his place. Having reached the top of the hill, which, as Bede puts it, was 'clad in a gay mantle of many kinds of flowers', St Alban asked God to give him water – a spring instantly bubbled at his feet. St Alban was beheaded on the hill, 'its beauty providing a worthy place to be hallowed by a martyr's blood', and as his head fell, the executioner's eyes dropped out to the ground. The converted headsman, known as St Heraclius, also suffered that day, being baptised in his own blood and recorded ever since in the Roman Martyrology.

St Alban is the first British Christian that we know by name and possibly the earliest known Latin Christian of the European provinces. There may well have been other martyrs during the Romano-British period. The sixth-century monk/historian, St Gildas, reports that many suffered under Diocletian as well as during the Saxon invasions, when a thousand were supposedly massacred near Lichfield, which means 'field of the dead'. What is particularly striking with St Alban is the continuity and extent of his cult. According to Bede, the miracles had not ceased at St Alban's tomb from the time of his martyrdom until his own day. In 429, St Germanus, bishop of Auxerre, and St Lupus, the young bishop of Troyes, visited it during their mission against the heresy of Pelagius – the other famous Christian of Romano-British times. Bishop Germanus exchanged some relics of the apostles and martyrs for earth from the tomb, and several churches were dedicated to St Alban in Gaul.

The shrine of St Alban was visited by masses of pilgrims right up until the Reformation, occasionally fuelled by the dubious results of monastic archaeology – in 1177 the bones of St Amphibalus were supposedly discovered at Redbourn, followed by St Alban's original grave in 1257. Ely claimed a rival, dating back to the days of Abbot Frederick in the eleventh century, a claim unsurprisingly denied by the monks of St Albans. Although the relics have gone, the shrine at St Albans has been restored to its impressive medieval appearance with a canopy of embroidered red silk covering the pedestal.

NJS

Places to Visit: St Albans Abbey which is founded upon the hill where the martyrdom took place.

Further Reading:

Jacob, E. F., *Illustrations to the Life of St Alban*, 1924.

Lowe, W., *History of the Legend of St Alban*, Academic Journal Offprint from *Proceedings of the Society of Antiquaries*, London, 1914–1915.

Roberts, E., *The Hill of the Martyr: An Architectural History of St Albans Abbey*, The Book Castle, 1994.

Watkins, J., *The Alban Guide to the Cathedral and the Abbey Church and its Surroundings (St Albans)*, St Albans, H. A. Richardson, 1953.

June 22nd
Feast

STS JOHN FISHER & THOMAS MORE

I DIE the king's good servant, but God's first.

– Last words of St Thomas More

I AM come here to die for Christ's Catholic Church. And I thank God.

– Words of St John Fisher from the scaffold

THESE MOST FAMOUS of the Reformation martyrs were also the first to be canonised, being raised to the altars by Pope Pius XI in 1935; St Thomas More was proclaimed Patron of Statesmen on 5 November 2000, during the celebration of the Great Jubilee.

John Fisher

St John Fisher was born at Beverley, the son of a draper, and educated at Cambridge University from the age of fourteen. At Cambridge he flourished as a renowned scholar, being elected as a Fellow of Michaelhouse (now Trinity College) and ordained priest in 1491. As his reputation grew, he held a series of increasingly important appointments both within his college and within the university, being appointed Chancellor of the University in 1504, the same year he was consecrated as Bishop of Rochester.

Some years earlier, in 1502, he became chaplain to Lady Margaret Beaufort, the King's mother, also becoming in that year the first Lady Margaret

Professor of Divinity at Cambridge. Between them, they refounded the University both financially and academically. Fisher introduced Greek and Hebrew into the curriculum and invited the famous scholar Erasmus to lecture.

As Bishop of Rochester, England's smallest see, Fisher was ardent in his pastoral care and particularly noted for the power of his preaching. He complemented his scholarship with his devout life and was thus well equipped zealously to defend the Church and its Sacraments against Luther's attacks. Even Henry VIII boasted that no other realm could claim such a distinguished prelate. During this time Fisher had been appointed chaplain to Henry VIII's wife, Catherine of Aragon.

As one of the king's most admired bishops, John Fisher had no escape from clearly declaring his mind with regards to the validity of King Henry's marriage. To do so made him a marked man. The matter first arose regarding the nullity suit of 1529, but it was not until 1534 that all public officials were required to swear to a form that the marriage of Henry and Catherine was illegal and invalid. Bishop Fisher, alone among the English bishops, was unable to do this, although he declared that he would be willing to swear allegiance to the succession of the children of Anne Boleyn. For this he was condemned to imprisonment in the Tower of London. In the intervening years between 1529 and 1534, he had protested against the title 'Head of the Church of England' for Henry VIII and had qualified it with the words 'so far as the law of God allows'. Earlier in 1534, before he was presented with the Oath of Succession, he had been threatened with imprisonment for the alleged encouragement of Elizabeth Barton, a young nun of Kent, who claimed to have been granted visions which prophesied divine retribution for King Henry if he divorced Catherine and married Anne Boleyn.

Imprisoned in the Tower, Fisher was deprived of the University Chancellorship and the See of Rochester. For a bishop of genuine asceticism, his letter to Thomas Cromwell, the Secretary of Henry VIII, makes poignant reading, so utterly deprived had the bishop been of clothes and food. But most cruel of all was his deprivation from receiving the sacraments and any priestly visitation.

The final days of his earthly life were marked by the newly elected Pope Paul III creating Fisher a cardinal. To many this has seemed a politically inept move – Henry responded by vowing that Fisher's head would be off before the Cardinal's hat would be on – but if the scarlet cardinalatial robes are supposed to remind the wearer of his promise to defend the Church to the spilling of his blood, then the honour bestowed on Fisher was indeed a timely one. Fisher was ready for this self-sacrifice.

On 22nd June, 1535, John Fisher was taken from the Tower to the scaffold on Tower Hill. Pardoning his executioner and clearly announcing that he was dying for the faith of the Catholic Church, he asked those nearby to pray for him. Praying the *Te Deum* and a psalm, he rested his head on the block and, with a single blow of the axe, he died.

Fisher's body was buried in the churchyard of All Hallows at Barking, but was soon exhumed and taken to be buried with the body of Thomas More in the chapel of the Tower in order to deter people from regarding his grave as the shrine of a saint. For a fortnight his head was displayed on London Bridge before being thrown into the Thames.

Thomas More

Being held in the Tower at the same time as John Fisher was Sir Thomas More, also a former man of state whom Henry VIII raised up only to throw down again.

Thomas More was son of Sir John More, one of the Justices of the King's Bench. He was born in 1478 in London. At the age of thirteen he was taken into the household of John Morton, the Archbishop of Canterbury (from 1486 to 1500) from whence he was sent to Canterbury College, Oxford (now incorporated into Christ Church). After returning to London to read Law at Lincoln's Inn, he was called to the Bar in 1501. Three years later More entered Parliament.

Before marrying Jane Colt in 1505, More had seriously considered whether or not he was called to the religious life. During this time he lived for four years at the London Charterhouse. Although he decided that his was not a vocation to a religious order, for the rest of his life More embraced many pious practices such as wearing a hairshirt and reciting the Little Office.

Jane More died in 1511, leaving Thomas with three daughters and one son. He remarried only a few weeks later, taking for his second wife Alice Middleton, who had herself lost her first spouse. The family life of the More household is legendary, immortalised by the famous painting by Hans Holbein. Thomas was as good a father as he was a lawyer, known for his strong commitment to the responsibilities of the former, as he was renowned for his integrity with regards to the duties of the latter. But it was his professional qualities that quickly came to the attention of the newly crowned Henry VIII, and thus Thomas rose swiftly in public office until in 1529 he succeeded the ill-fated Cardinal Wolsey as Lord Chancellor of England.

Throughout this time, More's reputation as a man of letters increased around Europe. Most notably his book *Utopia* was translated from the original Latin into the principal European languages. His wit and wisdom, however, was completely full of common sense, and if anyone was fooled by King Henry's munificence, More was not. 'If my head would win him a castle in France', he said, 'it should not fail to go.'

It was for no castle, however, that More's demise was to come about, but for the same reasons, with much the same chronology, that John Fisher (whom More greatly admired) came to his earthly end. Having resigned the Lord Chancellorship, More was impounded in the Tower on 13th April 1534, his lands confiscated and his family impoverished. Fifteen months later, on 1st July, he emerged from the Tower, a shadow of his former self, to be tried at Westminster Hall. He gave a robust defence, but was sentenced to death, a sentence executed on Tower Hill, on 6th July 1535, by beheading. To his beloved daughter, Meg, he wrote, 'Farewell my dear child, and pray for me, and I shall for you and all your friends, that we may merrily meet in heaven.' As he mounted the scaffold his last words were that he died for the faith of the Holy Catholic Church and was 'the king's good servant, but God's first'.

GS

Places to Visit: The Tower of London, where both were imprisoned, and nearby Tower Hill where the executions took place. The seminary of Allen Hall is built upon the site of the More family home, and the nearby church where the saint worshipped preserves a monument of him. Rochester Cathedral was the Episcopal See of St John Fisher.

Further Reading:

Fisher, St John, *Commentary on the Seven Penitential Psalms*, San Francisco, Ignatius Press, 2000.

Ackroyd, P., *The Life of Thomas More*, London, Chatto & Windus, 1998.

Beahn, J. E., *A Man Born Again: Saint Thomas More*, Milwaukee, Bruce Publishing Co, 1954.

Bridgett, T. E., *Life and Writings of Sir Thomas More, Lord Chancellor of England and Martyr under Henry VIII*, 1892.

Davies, M., *Saint John Fisher*, Long Prairie, MN, Neumann Press, 2001.

Hollis, C., *St Thomas More*, Burns and Oates, 1961.

McCann, Paul, *A Valiant Bishop Against a Ruthless King: The Life of St John Fisher*, St Louis, B. Herder Book Co., 1938.

Roper, W., *Life of Sir Thomas More*, Springfield, Templegate Publishers, 1983.

Reynolds, E. E., *The Field is Won*, Burns and Oates, 1968.

Reynolds, E. E., *Saint John Fisher*, Anthony Clarke Books, 1972.

Sargent, D., *Thomas More*, Sheed & Ward, 1940.

Surtz, E., 'Works and Days of John Fisher – An Introduction to the Position of St John Fisher (1469–1535), Bishop of Rochester', in *The English Renaissance and the Reformation*, Cambridge, MA, Harvard University Press, 1967.

Wegemer, G., *Thomas More: A Portrait of Courage*, Scepter, 1995.

June 23rd
Optional Memorial

St Etheldreda

QUEENLY by birth, an earthly crown she wore
Right nobly; but a heavenly pleased her more.
Scorning the marriage bed, a virgin wife
Twelve years she reigned, then sought a cloistered life.

– From Bede's *Hymn in Honour of St Etheldreda*

ST ETHELDREDA, also known as Audrey, is one of the most famous of a long series of royal Saxon saints who founded monasteries during the seventh and eighth centuries. Indeed, some of these belonged to her family. Her sisters included St Sexburga, Queen of Kent and founder of the nunnery of Minster-in-Sheppey, and St Withburga, founder of the nunnery at East Dereham in Norfolk. Moreover, St Etheldreda was sister to St Erconwald, founder of religious houses at Chertsey and Barking, and Bishop of London.

St Etheldreda was born at Exning, Suffolk, during the second quarter of the seventh century. Her father, Anna, became King of East Anglia at some point after her birth, and was killed by King Penda of Mercia in 654. We know very little about the short reign of Anna, but we do know something of his uncle, Redwald, who had been the most powerful ruler of his day, and was probably buried at Sutton Hoo. This burial site was discovered in 1939, revealing an unsurpassed collection of seventh-century treasures, including gold shoulder clasps, a large silver dish and a magnificent helmet. St Etheldreda's background was therefore both noble and saintly.

It is not surprising that, being a princess, St Etheldreda was expected to marry well, and so, as a young girl, she was betrothed to Tonbert, ealdorman of the Southern Gryvii. The marriage, which remained unconsummated, only lasted a couple of years, and after the death of Tonbert, St Etheldreda lived in solitude upon the Isle of Ely, which had been her dowry. However, political expediency intervened, and in 652 she married Egfrith, King of Northumbria (670–85). Knowing her desire for the convent, he reluctantly agreed that they could live as brother and sister, but after twelve years he grew tired of this arrangement and, upon the advice of Bishop Wilfrid of Northumbria, the unconsummated marriage was dissolved. Egfrith married again shortly afterwards. The new Queen took a dislike to Bishop Wilfrid, one of the reasons for his subsequent exile from Northumbria. Egfrith's death in battle at Nechtansmere (685) was seen as a punishment for turning against the saint.

St Etheldreda took the veil and withdrew to the monastery of Coldingham, on the Scottish border, founded by Egfrith's aunt, St Ebba the Elder. Shortly afterwards, she left the north for her East Anglian homeland, where she founded a double monastery on the Isle of Ely. Here she restored an ancient church, reputedly destroyed by the same pagan King Penda who had killed her father. As can be seen, royal and noble patronage were crucial in the growth of monasticism during the period. This growth was rapid. By the time of the first Viking raids at the end of the eighth century, there were well over 200 monastic communities in England. Links also continued with continental foundations – St Etheldreda's mother, St Hereswitha, and sister, St Ethelburga, joined the French houses at Chelles and Faremoutier respectively.

St Etheldreda spent her last seven years at Ely, living a life of prayer and penitence. We read that she ate once daily, always wore woollen clothes, and spent much of the night in prayer. Finally, in 679, the monastery was struck down with the dreaded plague. The holy Abbess developed a painful swelling on her neck, just under the jaw, which she regarded as a chastisement for her earlier love of richly jewelled necklaces. 'I realise very well', she said, 'that I deserve this wearisome disease in my neck, on which, as I well remember, when I was a girl, I used to wear the needless burden of jewellery . . . So now I wear a burning red tumour on my neck instead of gold and pearls'. Indeed, it is thought that the word 'tawdry', meaning showy, worthless finery, comes from the poor quality 'St Audrey's lace' sold at St Audrey's fair – a memory of the saint's love for extravagant neckwear. After a lingering illness and a painful operation on the tumour, she died on 23rd June, 679.

After her death, the family connections continued at Ely. Her sister, St Sexburga, succeeded her as Abbess, who in turn was followed by her daughter, St Ermengilda. Abbess Sexburga translated her sister's body to a new shrine on 17th October, 695. When her tomb was opened, St Etheldreda's body was found to be incorrupt and her neck completely healed. Her tomb became an important centre of pilgrimage, and she became the most popular of the Saxon women saints.

The Danes sacked the monastery in 870, and a century later St Ethelwold refounded it as a Benedictine house. Then one of the wealthiest abbeys in England, the building of the present cathedral was begun about 1080, and in 1106 the remains of St Etheldreda, St Sexburga, St Ermengilda and St Withburga (whose body had been stolen by the monks of Ely from Dereham) were enshrined at the East End. These were destroyed in 1541, although the Catholic Church in Ely claims the hand of St Etheldreda, discovered in Sussex in 1811, having probably been hidden by a recusant devotee of the saint. Not surprisingly, given the manner of her death, St Etheldreda is considered a patron for throat and neck ailments. She is also the patroness of the fenland University of Cambridge, paralleling the patroness of Oxford – St Frideswide, another royal foundress.

NJS

Places to Visit: Ely Cathedral, and the Catholic church of St Etheldreda at Ely Place, London.

Further Reading:

Stranks, C. J., *St Etheldreda, Queen and Abbess*, Ely Cathedral Monographs, 1975.

Caldecott, M., *Etheldreda, Princess of East Anglia, Queen of Northumbria, Saint of Ely*, Arkana, 1987.

Sneesby, N., *Etheldreda: Princess, Queen, Abbess and Saint*, Fern House, 1999.

July 1st
Optional Memorial

St Oliver Plunkett

I do forgive all who had a hand directly or indirectly in my death and in my innocent blood.

– **Last words of St Oliver from the scaffold**

OLIVER PLUNKETT was born of a noble, royalist family at Loughcrew in County Meath in 1629. At the age of eighteen, he accompanied, along with four others, the remarkable soldier turned Oratorian priest, Fr. Francis Scarampi, in order to travel to Rome to train for the priesthood. In May 1647, the group arrived in Rome, and the young Oliver was not to see Ireland again for the next twenty-three years.

Having arrived in the eternal city, Oliver commenced a brilliant academic career at the Irish College, becoming, after his priestly ordination in 1654, professor of theology at Propaganda College as well as working in Rome on behalf of the Irish bishops.

In 1669 he was appointed as Archbishop of Armagh, being consecrated in Ghent on 23rd November of that year. Plunkett continued to journey towards Ireland via London, where he was greeted favourably by Charles II's queen, Catherine of Braganza. When he finally arrived in Ireland, he set about the challenge of pastoral care for his people with immense zeal and energy, confirming nearly 50,000 people in his first four years of primacy while visiting his diocese. Almost immediately upon arriving in Ireland he held a synod which was intended to correct abuses, and was careful to draw up an address of loyalty to the King whilst at the same time giving guiding principles as to how being Catholic should form their attitudes with regards to civil power. Education was another field of great concern to the Archbishop, particularly regarding the training of future priests.

Towards the end of 1673, persecution of Catholics once more increased due to Puritan pressure upon the King. In Scotland and England a series of laws was promulgated, designed to suppress Catholic life and worship. The Irish government was instructed to pass a law which banished all bishops and religious orders from the country. But it was not until after this second synod in 1678 that, by order of the King and Council, Peter Talbot, the Archbishop of Dublin, then almost a dying man, had been arrested, and all the other Irish bishops banished. These were the repercussions from the so-called popish plot alleged by Titus Oates.

On 6th December 1679, Plunkett was arrested and incarcerated in Dublin Castle. At first he was charged with plotting to bring 20,000 French soldiers into Ireland and with levying taxes to support an army of 70,000 men. This was a ludicrous charge which was subsequently changed to the accusation of his setting up a false religion, a charge that, with the assistance of two former friars, was to send Plunkett to his death.

The sentence of being hanged, drawn and quartered was carried out on 1st July 1681, at Tyburn, Plunkett's body being afterwards taken to Lambspring Abbey in 1684. His body is now enshrined at Downside Abbey in Somerset, while his head is held in the Oliver Plunkett memorial church at Drogheda in County Louth. He was canonized by Pope Paul VI in 1976.

Dr. Brenan (Bishop of Waterford), a close friend of Archbishop Plunkett, wrote these lines after Plunkett's execution: 'In truth, his holy life merited for him this glorious death; during his twelve years of residence here he showed himself vigilant, zealous, and indefatigable above his predecessors, nor do we find within the memory of this present century that any Primate or Metropolitan visited his diocese and province with the same solicitude and pastoral zeal.'

GS

Places to Visit: The body of the saint can be venerated at Downside Abbey in Somerset, and his head at the Oliver Plunkett memorial church at Drogheda in Ireland.

Further Reading:

Curtayne, A., *The Trial of Oliver Plunkett,* Sheed and Ward, 1953.

Forristal, D., *Oliver Plunkett in His Own Words,* Dublin, Veritas Publications, 1975.

Hanly, J., *Oliver Plunkett,* Dublin, Veritas Publications, 1975.

McKee, J., *A Martyr Bishop: the Life of St Oliver Plunkett,* Lumen Christi Press, Houston, 1975.

Meagher, J., *Saint Oliver Plunkett,* Dublin, Irish Messenger Publications, 1975.

Stokes, J. F., *Life of Blessed Oliver Plunkett, Archbishop of Armagh (1625–1681),* Dublin, Catholic Truth Society, 1963.

July 11th
Feast

St Benedict

IF YOU are really a servant of Jesus Christ, let the chain of love hold you firm in your resolve, not a chain of iron.

– From the Rule of St Benedict

BENEDICT WAS BORN of a noble family in Norcia, central Italy, in the year 480. He studied literature at Rome, but it seems that, amid the decadence of the great city, he experienced a desire for solitude and the love of God. Abandoning his studies, he went away to live as a hermit in the neighbourhood of Subiaco, about forty miles from Rome. Here he lived in a cave perched on the side of a mountain and was fed each day by a loaf of bread lowered to him on a rope. But he was not to remain in this solitude for very long. Even in this inaccessible place his evident holiness attracted disciples and admirers, and before long he was asked to become abbot of a local monastery. He accepted, but was so zealous and strict as superior that the rebellious monks attempted to poison him. Miraculously, when Benedict blessed the poisoned cup before drinking from it, the vessel cracked from side to side and so he was saved. For this reason, one of St Benedict's symbols in art is a broken cup. Unsurprisingly, after this experience, Benedict gave up being abbot and returned to his cave. Still new disciples came to him, so he founded his own monastery in which he could promote his own ideal form of monasticism without opposition. This was the origin of the famous monastery of Subiaco, which still exists today, as does the Sacro Speco (Holy Cave) where Benedict first lived as a hermit.

Benedict attracted many holy men to Subiaco, among them Sts Maurus and Placidus, great saints of the Benedictine calendar. But he also attracted jealousy, including that of a local priest. This priest went so far as to try and create scandal for Benedict by dancing naked in the monastery, and generally created so much difficulty that Benedict was forced to make another move. This time he settled his followers on Monte Cassino, a tall hill-top south of Rome, and there grew up the mother house of the Benedictine movement, and one of the greatest monasteries in Europe. It was here at Monte Cassino that Benedict spent the remainder of his life, though he continued to travel from time to time, often to visit other monasteries and inspire them to a holier way of life.

Another visit, which he used to make annually, was to his sister (perhaps his twin sister), Scholastica. She too had embraced the religious life, and was abbess of her own convent. Every year the siblings used to meet in a little house halfway between their two monasteries and enjoy a day of conversation. On the last such occasion, Scholastica begged Benedict to stay the night with her as well, but he refused since it was his duty to return home every evening to his monastery. Upon this, Scholastica prayed to God, and so great a storm came down that it was impossible for Benedict to travel, and so he was forced to remain the night there after all. Three days later Scholastica died, and Benedict had her buried in his abbey at Monte Cassino. A few years later he died as well, and was buried in the same tomb as his sister.

It was while at Monte Cassino that St Benedict composed his famous 'Rule', the basis of the Benedictine life the whole world over. In modern times it has been shown that Benedict based his rule on another, earlier work called 'The Rule of the Master'. But this does not diminish his achievement. For although Benedict may have taken much of the content of his rule from the *Regula Magistri*, it was he who turned those individual elements into a workable, adaptable way of life. It is a way of life which has helped many thousands of souls to seek God, and, almost by accident, it has provided the order and stability necessary for the construction of true culture, for the cultivation of learning and the passing on of tradition. As Dom David Knowles has written, though we should consider the disciples of St Benedict first and foremost as followers of Christ, 'we may consider them also as a great cultural force, as the greatest single factor in transmitting the legacy of the past, as an important factor in the higher education of the renaissance of the twelfth century, as patrons of architecture and sculpture, as the only artists in calligraphy and illumination during the greater part of the Middle Ages.' For this contribution to Western civilisation, Benedict was declared the patron saint of Europe by Pope Paul VI on 24th October 1964.

RW

Places to Visit: South of Rome can be found St Benedict's first monastic site of Subiaco and also the great Monastery of Monte Cassino where his tomb is preserved.

Further Reading:

Cabrol OSB, F., *Saint Benedict*, London, Burns, Oates and Washbourne, 1934.

Camm, B., chapter on St Benedict in *Pilgrim Paths in Latin Lands*, MacDonald and Evans, 1923.

Lindsay, T. F., *Saint Benedict: His Life and Work*, London, Burns and Oates, 1949.

von Matt, L.; Hilpisch OSB, S., *Saint Benedict*, London, Burns and Oates, 1961.

Maynard, T., *St Benedict and his Monks*, Catholic Book Club, 1945.

July 23rd
Feast

St Bridget of Sweden

MY LORD Jesus, you are truly the head of all men and angels, the worthy King of kings and Lord of lords; and you do all your works out of true and ineffable love.

– **With such words St Bridget of Sweden addressed Christ**

BRIDGET, for many centuries patroness of her home country of Sweden and now a patron of Europe too, was born around 1302 or 1303. She was the daughter of Birger, the governor of Upland, and his second wife Ingebord. They were an important family, and Bridget herself was soon to be moving among the highest circles of Swedish society. Yet, from an early age, her principal concern was with the things of heaven. A devout child, she received visions and revelations from God at the age of seven, and these increased and multiplied as the years went on. But she was not called, at this stage of her life, to remove herself from the secular world and seek God alone in the solitude of the cloister. Instead, aged only fourteen, she was married to a nobleman called Ulf Gudmasson, with whom she was to raise a family of eight children. In 1341 Bridget and her husband made a great pilgrimage to Santiago de Compostela. She also became lady-in-waiting to Queen Blanche, wife of Magnus II the young king of Sweden, and sought to encourage the royal couple in their practice of the Christian faith, which she did with considerable success.

In 1344 Ulf died, and the widowed Bridget began to live the life of a penitent. Her visions and revelations became more frequent and began to be written down. In 1346, King Magnus founded a monastery at Vadstena, which became the mother house of the Bridgettine Order (officially called the Order of the Most Holy Saviour). Its special characteristic was that it was a double monastery, comprising houses for both men and women under the rule of a single superior, the abbess. This became characteristic of Bridgettine convents everywhere. Despite receiving this royal encouragement, the new order was not yet officially approved by the Church, so in 1349 Bridget travelled to Rome, partly to facilitate such approval. In fact, she was to remain in Rome for the rest of her life. The order was officially approved in 1370, and the first abbess of Vadstena was Bridget's own daughter, now known as St Catherine of Sweden.

In Rome, Bridget's mystical life continued. She received visions of the passion of Christ and of important future events. Perhaps inspired by the Jubilee of 1350, she was known to make many pilgrimages to the holy places within Rome and throughout Italy. But she was involved too in very practical work with the poor and the humble, with all those in need. The English mystic Margery Kempe met Bridget's maid, who has left a charming description of the saint. 'She was kind and meek to every creature, and had a laughing face'. Yet at the same time Bridget could mix with the most powerful leaders of Christendom, who respected her and listened to her advice. She could discuss politics with kings and princes, and ecclesiastical reform with abbots and bishops. In particular, she urged the popes, who were then living at Avignon, to return to their proper place in Rome. She died too soon to see this happen, but continued to work and pray for it until the day she died. Her death finally came in 1373, after a long pilgrimage to the Holy Land. Her sanctity was recognised immediately, and in less than twenty years she was canonised, by Pope Boniface IX in 1391. Although she is still venerated in her preserved room at the Bridgettine convent in Rome, her relics constitute a rare and precious Swedish shrine at Vadstena.

For her counsel to the leaders of nations, and the influence for the good which she was able to bring, Bridget was declared a patron saint of Europe by Pope John Paul II in October 1999. He wrote, 'She stands as an important witness to the place reserved in the Church for a charism lived in complete docility to the Spirit of God and in full accord with the demands of ecclesial communion'.

RW

Places to visit: Her rooms can be visited just off the Piazza Farnese in Rome, and her relics are kept in the Lutheran shrine at Vadstena in Sweden.

Further Reading:

St Bridget of Sweden, *Revelations of St Bridget*, Rockford, IL, TAN Publishing Company, 1984.

Anderson, A., *Saint Bridget of Sweden: Patroness of Europe*, London, CTS, 1980.

Jørgensen, J.; Lund, I. (trans.), *Saint Bridget of Sweden*, London, Longmans Green, 1954.

Kezel, A. R. (trans.); Harris, M. T. (ed.), *Birgitta of Sweden: Life and Selected Writings*, New York, Paulist Press, 1990.

Peacey, E., *Saint Birgitta of Sweden*, 1934.

Redpath, H., *God's Ambassadress, St Bridget of Sweden*, Milwaukee, Bruce Publishing Co., 1947.

August 9th
Feast

St Teresa Benedicta of the Cross (Edith Stein)

ONE can only learn the science of the cross by feeling the cross in one's own person.
– From *The Science of the Cross* by Edith Stein

AS CLOSELY AS St Thérèse of the Child Jesus configured her life to her religious name, so too did Edith Stein on taking her religious name, Teresa Benedicta of the Cross, configure her life to the ultimate level humanly possible, offering her very life to Christ.

Edith Stein was born in Breslau (Germany) on 12th October 1891, of Jewish parents, Siegfried Stein and Auguste Courant. Early in her teens, Edith completely lost faith in the idea of God, but yet retained a passionate desire for truth and led a life of high moral standards. From the start of her education she demonstrated a precocious gift for learning, immersing herself in the world of philosophy.

In 1913, Edith went to the University of Göttingen to study under, and eventually to assist, the great philosopher Edmund Husserl. It was during her time at Göttingen that she first came into contact with living Christianity. She had been asked to help the widow of the philosopher Adolf Reinach to sort out his papers. Being very sensitive herself, she dreaded the task, knowing that the Reinachs' marriage had been blissfully happy until Adolf was killed in war in November 1917. However, the Reinachs had become Christian a year before Adolf's death, and the widow was not only strong in herself but a source of consolation for others. This experience made a deep impression on Edith, as did the return to the Catholic faith of the philosopher Max Scheler, whom she had first met in 1913.

The ground prepared, it was St Teresa of Avila, the great reformer of the Carmelite order, who guided Edith to the Church of Christ. One evening, whilst she was staying at a friend's house, Edith happened to pick up a copy of the Life of St Teresa; indeed, it was the Spanish mystic's autobiography. She started to read and could not put the book down until the small hours of the morning. Profoundly moved, Edith believed she had found the truth she had been searching for. She would comment years later, 'Whoever seeks the truth is seeking God, whether consciously or unconsciously'. On New Year's Day 1922, she was baptised.

Soon after her conversion she abandoned her academic career, devoting herself entirely to prayer and teaching in a Dominican school at Speyer. But quickly she was drawn to the writings of St Thomas Aquinas, translating his work De Veritate into German. This short renewal of her academic career was cut short by the rising Nazi intolerance of 'non-Aryans' in educational fields.

On 14th October 1933, Edith Stein entered the discalced Carmelite community at Cologne-Lindenthal. The following April she received the habit and the new name Sister Teresa Benedicta of the Cross, making her final profession of vows on Easter Sunday 1935. As a sister in Cologne she was admired for her great humility and her ardent devotion to the Eucharist, sometimes praying for hours at a time. However, the clouds of war and persecution were gathering. In November 1938, it was decided that not only she but the whole community was in danger due to her presence as a Jewish-born nun. On New Year's Eve she was taken to the Carmelite convent at Echt in neutral Holland. On Passion Sunday 1939, she offered herself 'to the Heart of Jesus as a sacrifice of expiation for true peace, that the reign of the Antichrist may perish'. This was now her mission until the end of her earthly life.

In Echt, Sister Teresa Benedicta continued to write theological works until, on the evening of 2nd August 1942, the Germans having now invaded

Holland, the Gestapo came and arrested her as part of the Nazi reprisal for an outspoken pastoral letter of the Dutch bishops condemning the persecution of the Jews. At first she was taken to the concentration camp at Westerbork, but five days later she and many others were transported by cattle truck to Auschwitz. Some prisoners released later from Westerbork wrote of Sister Teresa Benedicta's great calm and charity during her time there, especially towards the children whose own mothers were beside themselves with fear. Two days after arriving at Auschwitz, 9th August 1942, she was sent to the gas chambers.

At the time of her arrest she had been working on a book entitled *The Science of the Cross* in which she wrote, 'One can only learn the science of the cross by feeling the cross in one's own person.'

Pope John Paul II beatified Teresa Benedicta of the Cross during a pastoral visit to Cologne on 1st May 1987, canonising her in Rome on 11th October 1998. The following year the Pope declared her one of the Patrons of Europe, saying, 'She has thus become the symbol of a human, cultural and religious pilgrimage which embodies the deepest tragedy and the deepest hopes of Europe.'

GS

Places to Visit: Auschwitz, the place of her martyrdom, and the Carmelite community house at Cologne-Lindenthal where she spent her religious life.

Further Reading:

Collected Works of Edith Stein, Washington DC, ICS Publications, 1986–.

Bordeaux, H., *Edith Stein: Thoughts on Her Life and Times*, Milwaukee, 1959.

de Fabrègues, Jean; trans. Antoine, D. M., *Edith Stein: Philosopher, Carmelite Nun, Holocaust Martyr*, New York, Alba House, 1965.

Gaboriau, F.; trans. McInerny, R., *The Conversion of Edith Stein*, St Augustine's Press, 2002.

Graef, H. C., *The Scholar and the Cross: The Life and Works of Edith Stein*, New York, Longmans and Green, 1955.

Herbstrith, W.; trans. Bonowitz, B., *Edith Stein: A Biography*, San Francisco, Ignatius Press, 1992.

August 26th
Optional Memorial

Bl Dominic of the Mother of God

IS THERE any hope, that I shall cross the sea and convey my body to that island to which twenty-two years ago I sent my heart?

– Blessed Dominic writing about England in one of his letters

ONE OF THE GREAT surprises in the salvation history of nineteenth-century England is the sudden arrival of the simple saintly figure of Dominic Barberi. His arrival coincides with the period called by Newman 'The Second Spring', when the Catholic Church in England was unexpectedly resurrected after three centuries of persecution and progressive diminution. Barberi has been aptly called 'the shepherd of the second spring' as he guided many into the one fold of Christ and won a new appreciation for Catholicism in England. He came as a prophet sent by a divine call to preach a message of conversion, to awaken an apathetic and sceptical age to the reality of its divine vocation.

He was born in the papal city of Viterbo, of farming stock. Despite having few opportunities for education, he had an innate desire for learning and taught himself to read. Through lack of guidance in his early years, he fell under some unhealthy influences from bad books and company which almost stole him away from his original desire to lead a consecrated life. After a great spiritual battle and two extraordinary visions of hell, he surrendered to the call of God. Despite not having sufficient formal education, he was accepted into the Passionist novitiate to train as a brother. His outstanding qualities of virtue and intellect were soon noticed, and against all precedent he was transferred to priestly training.

St Paul of the Cross, the founder of the Passionist Congregation, had been given visions about the conversion of England, and had seen his own religious sons playing a great part. St Paul had prayed every day of his life for the conversion of England and this had become a particular Passionist concern. Yet the congregation had as yet not set foot on the shores of Britain. Like his holy Father, Blessed Dominic was granted prophetic visions in both 1813 and 1814, in which he was told of his own mission to England. This concern, given to him supernaturally for a country he knew not, became his abiding preoccupation.

A few years after his ordination in 1818, he became professor and director of students at Sant'Angelo and then at Rome. He was a prodigious writer and produced several works, including manuals of philosophy and of moral theology. In 1831 he became superior of the Passionist house in Lucca and the provincial of all southern Italy. Yet his desire to go to England was continually thwarted by circumstances beyond his control, namely his superiors and his poor health. He had met some convert Englishmen in Rome, including the Venerable Ignatius Spencer, with whom he began to correspond. He also gathered a group of devout souls to pray and make sacrifices for the English mission. He grew in holiness and the mystical way of St Paul of the Cross during many years of trial. He grew particularly close to the Virgin Mary, and was granted many visions of her. It was from this special relationship that he came to be known as 'Dominic of the Mother of God'.

Finally, he was given news that he was to lead a new mission to northern Europe and set up a new foundation in Belgium. He set off with a small band of missionaries from the Caelian Hill in Rome, just as St Augustine had begun in 596. He made his first trip to England in November 1840. Then in October of the following year he returned for good.

His first months in England were very difficult. He could hardly speak the language and the people were either apathetic or hostile. At Aston in Staffordshire, he established a first monastery in February 1842. At nearby Stone, people jeered and ridiculed him, throwing stones which he would only pick up and kiss in return. Eventually, through his goodness, he won many around, and his work of preaching missions in parishes became very successful. Seven years later his remains would pass through Stone with admirers and devotees lining the streets.

On the cold, wet, wintry night of 8th October 1845, he was called to meet John Henry Newman at his retreat of discernment in Littlemore. They had met before, and Newman had been touched by Dominic's 'Lament over England' in which he adapted the lamentation of Jeremiah over the state of Jerusalem to the contemporary situation in England. Newman's difficulty had been in seeing the mark of holiness in the Church of Rome. In Dominic he clearly saw this and was received into full communion with the Catholic Church. Newman would later write: 'Father Dominic played a great part in my own conversion and that of others. His very look had about it something holy. When his form came within sight, I was moved to the depths in the strangest way'. It was not by chance that Blessed Dominic brought to completion a journey which represented, in the words of Pope Paul VI, 'The most meaningful, the most conclusive, that human thought ever travelled during the last century, indeed one might say during the modern era, to arrive at the fullness of wisdom and of peace'.

The Passionist community continued to grow and new foundations were made. Dominic's years in England, though, would be short. His health was always weak, and before long it would fail him. He had worn himself out for his beloved country. His visible achievement had been modest, yet his spiritual and moral influence had been incalculable. He collapsed at Pangbourne station on 27th August 1849, and died the following day at 3pm in the Railway Tavern at Reading.

He had written in 1836, 'Is there any hope, that I shall cross the sea and convey my body to that island to which twenty-two years ago I sent my heart?' His hope was fulfilled. He was finally laid to rest at the Passionist house in St Helens, where today his shrine can be visited. He is also venerated at the beautiful shrine at 'the College' at Littlemore near Oxford where he received Newman. He was beatified on 23rd October 1963 and the Church in England still awaits his canonisation. A. Wilson, the great biographer of

Blessed Dominic, wrote, 'In the whole of Christian hagiography it would, we think, be impossible to find a servant of God whose whole spiritual life was so entirely poised on zeal for the conversion of one country.'

MPH

Places to Visit: The shrine at St Helens, Lancashire, where his body is preserved. 'The College' at Littlemore near Oxford where he received John Henry Newman into the Catholic Church.

Further Reading:

Gwynn, D., *Father Dominic Barberi*, London, Burns & Oates, 1947.

Mead, J., *Shepherd of the Second Spring: The Life of Blessed Dominic Barberi, CP, 1792–1849*, Patterson, NJ, St Anthony Guild Press, 1968.

Wilson, A., *Blessed Dominic Barberi: Supernaturalized Briton*, Sands, 1967.

Young, U., *Life and Letters of the Venerable Father Dominic (Barberi) CP*, 1926.

August 30th
Optional Memorial

THE THREE WOMAN MARTYRS: STS MARGARET CLITHEROW, ANNE LINE, MARGARET WARD

I AM sentenced to die for harbouring a Catholic priest, and so far am I from repenting for having so done, that I wish, with all my soul, that where I have entertained one, I could have entertained a thousand.

– St Anne Line at her trial

ONLY THREE of the canonised martyrs of England and Wales are women, although undoubtedly many more women gave their lives either unto death or in a living martyrdom for the sake of the faith which they loved.

Margaret Clitherow

St Margaret Clitherow was described by contemporaries with great affection: 'everyone loved her and would run to her for help, comfort and counsel in distress.'

Margaret was born a Protestant in York in 1556, but three years after marrying John Clitherow, a lapsed Catholic, she met one of the first priests to return to England from the newly established seminary in Douai. That year, 1574, she became a Catholic, and she spent the next twelve years of her life sheltering and providing for the missionary priests.

In her home she set about instructing her own three children, and those of her Catholic neighbours, in the Faith, whilst all the time joyously and generously devoting herself to her family's domestic needs.

When a law was passed in 1585 making it a crime punishable by death for anyone to receive or relieve a priest, Margaret continued to offer her hospitality to the needy missionaries. In 1584 she secretly sent her eldest son, Henry, aged twelve, to the seminary at Douai. By 1586, Henry's absence was noted and Margaret's husband questioned. At the same time the house was raided. All remained faithful to Margaret and the authorities discovered nothing until they terrorised a Flemish boy of fourteen, who attended her school, into speaking. All was lost and everything found; priests' hiding places, vestments and hosts.

Margaret was immediately arrested and accused of 'harbouring Jesuits and seminary priests, traitors to the Queen's Majesty'. 'I have never harboured any but the Queen's friends', she replied. In fact, Margaret even refused to plead 'not guilty', saying, 'Having made no offence, I need no trial' – her purpose being to avoid the necessity of family, friends or servants being forced to give testimony against her; and to avoid involving a jury in the guilt of her death. The terrible penalty for refusing to plead was *peine forte et dure*, which resulted in the victim's being crushed to death.

On Friday 25th March, 1586, the young Margaret was taken from Ouse Bridge Prison barefoot to the Toll Booth, where, in the dungeons, she was stripped, laid on the floor in the manner of a cross, a sharp stone placed under her back and her body covered with a linen sheet. Upon her was placed a heavy wooden door onto which weights were stacked. Fifteen minutes later her agony ceased as she called out for the last time, 'Jesus, Jesus, Jesus, have mercy on me.' Her house in the Shambles in York is now a Catholic chapel and the relic of her hand is preserved in the old recusant Bar Convent.

Margaret Ward

Two years later, in 1588, Margaret Ward followed her sister in Christ to the heavenly banquet. She was born at Congleton in Cheshire, travelling to London to enter into the service of the Whittle family at an early age. This family, like Margaret Clitherow, protected Douai priests. One of them, William

Watson, was imprisoned in Bridewell prison. He was losing his mind due to suffering. Upon hearing of this, Margaret resolved to try to set him free.

Having befriended the gaoler's wife, Margaret succeeded in gaining access to the prisoner, bringing him food, drink and clothes. At last she managed to smuggle in a rope, and arranged for John Roche, an Irish boatman, to wait below the prison early one morning. Tragically, the escaping priest had doubled the rope; it therefore not being long enough, he left it hanging from his window and jumped, making some noise as he made good his escape.

The priest escaped, but it was quickly realised that the rope had been provided by Margaret. She and John Roche were arrested. Despite torture, Margaret refused to reveal where the priest might have gone into hiding. She also rejected an offer of freedom in return for conforming to the Church of England. On 29th August 1588, she was tried at the Old Bailey and sentenced to death. The very next day she was taken, with John Roche and with two other laymen and a priest, to Tyburn, singing as they went.

Anne Line

As Margaret Clitherow and Margaret Ward had assisted priests, so too did Anne Line give up her life for Christ and his Church.

Anne was born of ardent Calvinist parents, but both she and her brother were received into the Catholic Church before they had reached the age of twenty. Upon doing so they were both disinherited by their parents. At the age of nineteen, Anne married Roger Line, a convert like herself. But it was not long after their marriage that Roger was arrested and exiled to Flanders, where he died in 1594, leaving his wife completely unprovided for.

After finding shelter for a time in Essex, Anne became housekeeper to Fr. John Gerard, a priest who kept a large house in London which was used to shelter priests for varying periods of time. Despite almost continual ill-health, Anne was known for her hard work, her kindness and her generosity. She well knew the mortal danger in which she chose to live, many times telling Fr. Gerard, 'I naturally want more than anything to die for Christ'.

After Fr. Gerard's arrest, Anne moved to another house. At this time she took vows of poverty, chastity, and obedience. On Candlemas Day, 1601, Anne allowed an unusually large number of Catholics to attend Mass. Just as the Mass was about to begin the priest-hunters arrived at the heavily barred and bolted door. There was just enough time for the priest to take his vestments off and hide them before the pursuivants barged into the crowded room. Anne was arrested and taken to prison.

After a mockery of a trial at the Old Bailey, Anne Line was taken to Tyburn the following day, 27th February 1601. She joyously declared to the crowd her sentence, 'I am sentenced to die for harbouring a Catholic priest, and so far am I from repenting for having so done, that I wish, with all my soul, that where I have entertained one, I could have entertained a thousand.' Kissing the gallows, she then knelt down to pray, continuing to pray until the end.

GS

Places to visit: For Margaret Clitherow one can visit her house in the Shambles, York, which has been preserved as a Catholic shrine. Also her incorrupt hand is kept at the Bar Convent in York. For Margaret Ward and Anne Line one can visit the Martyrs' shrine at Tyburn Convent, (near Marble Arch) in London.

Further Reading:

Challoner, R., *Memoirs of Missionary Priests* (many editions). Contains all three martyrs.

Claridge, M., *Margaret Clitherow*, Burns and Oates, 1966.

Halley, S., *Margaret Clitherow*, London, Catholic Truth Society, 1980.

Reany, W., *Bl. Margaret Ward*, London, 1919.

Whatmore, L. E., *Blessed Margaret Ward*, Farm Street, 1969.

August 31st
Optional Memorial

St Aidan & the Saints of Lindisfarne

BROTHER, it seems to me that you were too severe on your ignorant hearers. You should have followed the practice of the Apostles, and begun by giving them the milk of simpler teaching, and gradually instructed them in the word of God until they were capable of greater perfection and able to follow the sublime precepts of Christ.

– **St Aidan's advice for the English mission (from Bede's *Ecclesiastical History*)**

UNDER THE SIGN of a wooden cross that he had erected before the battle of Heavenfield in 634, King Oswald, like a new Constantine, regained the kingdom of Northumbria for the royal dynasty of Bernicia. 'When the heavenly sign was set up, a heavenly victory won and heavenly wonders shown' it was, in the interpretation of the Venerable Bede, a portent of great things to come. During his many years of exile among the Irish, Oswald had grown familiar with the Christian faith under the influence of St Columba's missionary community of Iona. On becoming ruler his desire was to introduce this exemplary monastic tradition into Northumbria for the propagation of the Faith.

A renowned monk was sent from Iona with a small band of brethren. Yet this first mission failed to make any impact among the Anglo-Saxons, the monks finding the natives barbarous and pagan. During an important meeting about the future of the mission, the monks of Iona were struck by the wisdom of a young monk named Aidan. He appeared to have the tolerance and the skills necessary for such a task. So, rising from obscurity, he himself was sent.

He first sought out an island like Iona on which to form an ascetical monastic base. Off the north-eastern coast of England, he found Lindisfarne Island (now aptly called 'Holy Island'), a stretch of land which stood as a causeway on the river. It was perfectly placed in sight of the royal castle of Bamburgh. It was from here that St Aidan began the great evangelisation of the north. He had the constant support of King Oswald, who acted for some time as his interpreter.

Aidan founded other churches and monasteries in the region, and encouraged all people to follow simple lives of fasting and meditation. His own holiness and poverty enabled him to confront fearlessly the wealthy and powerful when necessary. During Lent he would go to the Farne Islands to live in solitude and greater poverty and penance. He was known for his many miracles and prophesies, some of which Bede records with great care.

After Oswald's death in 642, Aidan enjoyed the support and friendship of his successor Oswin. On one occasion, King Oswin gave him a fine royal horse only to find out later that Aidan had given it away to a poor man. The King was furious and questioned Aidan. The holy bishop responded, 'What are you saying, Your Majesty? Is this foal of a mare more valuable to you than a son of God?' After turning this over in his mind for some time, Oswin knelt at Aidan's feet and begged his forgiveness. Aidan later lamented to his chaplain, 'I know that the king will not live very long, for I have never seen so humble a king as he'.

For Bede, Aidan was the model bishop, 'In all that he believed, worshipped, and taught, his whole purpose was identical with our own, namely the redemption of the human race through the passion, resurrection, and ascension into heaven of the man Jesus Christ, the mediator between God and man'.

After an episcopate of 16 years, Aidan passed away on 31st August 651. That very day a shepherd boy on the surrounding hills saw a shaft of light rising over the church of Lindisfarne as a sign of the holy bishop's soul speeding upwards towards God. This boy was Cuthbert, who would one day continue the work of Aidan. St Aidan's body was laid to rest in the monks' cemetery on Lindisfarne, which soon became a hallowed place. St Aidan was the inspiration of many saints from the monastery of Lindisfarne who were to follow him.

After the Vikings sacked Lindisfarne, the shrine was destroyed and his cult diminished. In the 10th century, Glastonbury Abbey obtained some of the remaining relics and became the centre for his cult. Today Aidan is remembered once again on Lindisfarne Island, and a large bronze statue stands near to the site of his monastery, in memory of this great apostle.

MPH

Places to Visit: Holy Island, Lindisfarne and the Farne Islands in Northumberland permit an unspoilt impression of Aidan's original setting. One can also still see the monastic ruins.

Further Reading:

Adam, D., *Holy Island*, Norwich, Canterbury Press, 1997.

Backhouse, J., *The Lindisfarne Gospels*, Oxford, Phaidon, 1992.

Grierson, E., *The Story of the Northumbrian Saints*, London, A. R. Mowbray & Co., 1913.

Hume, B., *Footprints of the Northern Saints*, Darton, Longman and Todd, 1996.

Magnusson, M., *Lindisfarne: The Cradle Island*, Oriel Press, 1984.

Mayr-Harting, H., *The Coming of Christianity to Anglo-Saxon England*, Penn State Press, 1972.

September 3rd
Memorial

St Gregory the Great

MY very dear sons, it is better never to undertake any high enterprise than to abandon it when once begun.
– St Gregory writing to the first missionaries to England

FEW POPES have received the title of 'Great', yet Gregory's is surely the most undisputed. He ranks among a small number of saintly popes who have shaped the course of history. The now popular papal title 'Servant of the Servants of God' originated with him. His earliest biographers, Bede, Aldhelm and the anonymous author of Whitby, call him the 'Apostle of the English', 'our father and apostle in Christ', 'he from whom we have received the Christian faith, he who will present the English people to the Lord on the Day of Judgement as their teacher and apostle'.

Born into a Roman senatorial family around 540, Gregory was destined to play his role in government. He entered the service of the state as a young man. But his mind was set on higher things and, as Bede tells us, 'soaring above what is transitory' he chose to devote himself to all things spiritual. In 573 he sold his estates and founded six monasteries in Sicily and a seventh in Rome. A year later he entered the monastery which he had founded on the Caelian hill in Rome, on the site of his ancestral home. Here he lived a distinguished and highly ascetic existence.

At the command of Pope Benedict I, he was soon called out of the monastery to become one of the seven deacons of Rome. Pelagius II made him ambassador in Byzantium. He would lament 'My pastoral responsibilities now compel me to have dealings with worldly men, and when I recall my former peace, it seems that my mind is bespattered with this mire of daily affairs'. After six years he returned to his own monastery in order to become abbot. During this period he conceived of a mission to the new peoples of the ancient island of Britannia. It is here that we can best locate the traditional story that Bede so well records. On seeing Anglo-Saxon slaves for sale in the Roman markets, Gregory was struck by their appearance: 'Not Angles but angels', he said. He petitioned the Pope to send him to evangelise these people, yet with no success.

His monastic and missionary hopes were further dashed when he was elected pope during an outbreak of plague in Rome. Reluctantly, he submitted. It was a turbulent period for Rome, especially with the breakdown of imperial authority. Gregory had to take on many of the roles of a secular ruler. He established a peace with the threatening Lombards (592–593), appointed governors of Italian towns, and administered the vast estates of the Church. His careful protection of all the churches of the West and his missionary endeavours were quite remarkable at such a time, as was the preservation of good relations with the East. Maintaining, amidst such chaos, the independence of the Church, he is considered the father of medieval Christendom.

In the whole process of the mission to the Anglo-Saxons, Gregory took a personal lead. After he was inspired by meeting members of the race in Rome, he liberated them from slavery and led them to the monastic life. As pope he could finally initiate the mission to Britannia. He personally chose and sent out the monks from his own monastery for the voyage, and wrote letters before, during and after to gain support from Gaulish Christian rulers. When the monks, having arrived in Gaul, had fears and hesitations about continuing, he encouraged them, saying, 'My very dear sons, it is better never to undertake any high enterprise than to abandon it when once begun'. When they had arrived in Canterbury, he gave special advice to Augustine, sent reinforcements in 601 and also the Pallium, to establish the Church under Augustine with archiepiscopal authority. He also wrote to the King and Queen of Kent to urge them forward in the faith of Christ. This unique pastoral care was not only reciprocated by the English race in a special affection for Gregory himself but for his successors in the chair of Peter, as is evidenced in the history of the Anglo-Saxon Church.

Along with Ambrose, Jerome and Augustine, he is one of the four Latin Doctors of the Church. His writings have been influential from his time until our own. He had a huge literary output which is noted for its quality not only of content but of style. He was able to preserve and pass on the wisdom of the Fathers to the new world of the West that was quickly emerging as the old faded away. Apart from many biblical commentaries, he wrote an original work, *The Pastoral Care*, for rulers in the Church. He composed *The Dialogues* on the lives of the saints, as well as numerous letters which are of great historical value (854 of them are preserved).

He played a significant role in the development of the Roman liturgical rite. His prayers and compositions form the basis of the Gregorian Sacramentary. Having been involved in the codification and adaptation of various chant forms, the ancient chant of the Latin Church is now called 'Gregorian Chant' after him.

While his original monasticism probably owed more to the Basilian monastic tradition, he is rightly claimed by the Benedictine tradition as a father for his influence in what came to be the normative monastic tradition of the west. He wrote the first and most influential life of St Benedict, and *The Dialogues* reveal a great penetration of his rule.

He was around 65 years of age when he died in March 604, and was soon acclaimed a saint. His reign of just 13 years had a major influence on the history of Christendom. His tomb lies in St Peter's Basilica, close to the sacristy. Bede records his epitaph, where it is written, 'To Christ he led the Angles, and, by grace, to Faith and Church he added one race'.

MPH

Places to visit: His tomb lies in St Peter's Basilica in Rome, and the site of his monastic foundation is preserved around the Church of San Gregorio on the Caelian Hill.

Further Reading:

Almedingen, E., *St Gregory the Great*, Dublin, Irish Messenger, 1930.

Batiffol, P., trans. Stoddard, J. L., *Saint Gregory the Great*, Burns & Oates, 1929.

Gasquet, F. A., *A Life of Pope St Gregory the Great*, Westminster Art and Book Company, 1904.

Saxton, A. J., *St Gregory the Great*, London, Catholic Truth Society, 1927.

September 4th
Optional Memorial

St Cuthbert

PRESERVE amongst yourselves unfailing divine charity, and when you have to hold a council about your common affairs, let your principal aim be to reach a unanimous decision. Live in mutual concord with all other servants of Christ.

– From the last words of St Cuthbert, recorded in Bede's *Life of Cuthbert*

THIS COLOURFUL SAINT has often been aptly called the 'St Francis of England'. His popular appeal throughout the centuries is enormous, and the greatest testimony to this is the Cathedral of Durham, built to house his treasured shrine, which can still be seen today.

There are three lives of Cuthbert written within a very short period after his death, one by the monks of his monastery at Lindisfarne, the other two by Bede the Venerable. This puts his life in a privileged position with regard to the historian. We have more testimony about his life than any other saint of that period.

He was born into a humble family around 634. We are told that as a young boy he was set aside by the providence of God. He was playing with his friends when Christ appeared to him and told him that he was called to very great and noble things and should cease with his frivolity. One August night in 651, while looking after sheep, Cuthbert saw a great light ascending into heaven, as a sign of the death of St Aidan and his entrance into heaven. He was so moved by this experience that he joined the monastery of Melrose.

He found himself under the tutelage of St Eata and St Boisil. He went with Eata to make the new foundation of the monastery of Ripon. After the death of Boisil (c.661) he succeeded as Prior of Melrose and became renowned for his zeal for souls. He was known to journey to the remotest parts spreading the Gospel and ministering to the faithful.

Eventually Cuthbert was sent by Eata, by now a bishop, to be superior of the mother-house of Lindisfarne (663/4), the holy island where Aidan had first begun the conversion of the north. He managed to unite the house in adopting the Roman customs agreed upon at the Synod of Whitby. He himself however found the active life distasteful and continually sought out solitude whenever possible.

We are told by his biographers that he had a supernatural rapport with God's creation, especially the animal kingdom – something often reported of St Francis and many other saints. Once, having spent the whole night in prayer on the sea-shore, he was approached at dawn by two otters from the sea who warmed his frozen feet. On another occasion, on a missionary journey with a companion, they were without food when, at Cuthbert's request, an eagle soared overhead and dropped them a fish.

Cuthbert retired as prior in 676 and went to the small and barren Farne Islands, set off Lindisfarne, where Aidan had been known to spend the Lenten season. His brethren constructed here a little cell and an oratory. Here for 12 years Cuthbert lived a life absorbed in God, with only the birds of the air and fish of the sea as his companions. Yet he was disturbed by all and sundry who knew of his holiness and desired his counsel.

Under the instigation of Archbishop Theodore, it was decided that Cuthbert should be appointed a bishop. It took the personal intervention of King Egfrith of Northumbria and his attendants, who journeyed out to Cuthbert's hermitage, in order to persuade him. He was appointed Bishop of Hexham in 684, but soon after moved his diocese to Lindisfarne. He was known to be exemplary in preaching and teaching the holy faith and in visiting his diocese. Bede tells us that when he offered the sacrifice of the Mass he was known to cry. He attracted many through the beauty of his presentation of the gospel message. Many miracles and prophecies surround the accounts of this period.

When he saw that death was approaching he retired to his solitary island and passed from this world on 20th March 687. He had desired to be buried on his eremitical island, yet he was immediately taken to the Cathedral of Lindisfarne. He was moved again 11 years later due to increased veneration, and his body was found to be miraculously preserved. This began a remarkable series of removals and re-burials through which the cult of the saint survived.

In 875 the monks of Lindisfarne were driven away by the Danish invasions. The relics of Cuthbert were carried from place to place until they finally found their great resting place at Durham in 995. In 1104 his relics were again translated, this time to the new Norman Cathedral. After an originally sceptical examination they were once again found to be incorrupt to the surprise of many. From here the great medieval cult of Cuthbert developed to such a great scale. When the shrine was dismantled at the reformation, the body was still found to be in a remarkable state of preservation. From this point the history of the relics is clouded in mystery. It is claimed that recusants hid the body to protect it. The tradition today is that only three people know the whereabouts of Cuthbert's remains: the Abbot of Ampleforth and two others. Yet there are many precious contemporary and near contemporary secondary relics (clothes, vestments, the original coffin, portable altar and pectoral cross) which were found in Cuthbert's tomb during the 19th century, and can be seen in Durham today.

MPH

Places to visit: The monastic ruin and original setting of St Cuthbert on Holy Island, Lindisfarne. Durham Cathedral preserves his great shrine and in its treasury is contained many secondary relics of the saint.

Further Reading:

Adam, D., *Fire of the North*, London, SPCK, 1993.

Battiscombe, C. F. (ed.), *The Relics of Saint Cuthbert; Studies by Various Authors*, Oxford University Press, 1956.

Colgrave, H., *Saint Cuthbert of Durham*, G. Bailes and Sons, 1947.

Consitt, E., *Life of Saint Cuthbert*, Burns and Oates, 1887.

Hume, B., *Footprints of the Northern Saints*, DLT, 1996.

Mayr-Harting, H., *The Coming of Christianity to Anglo-Saxon England*, Penn State Press, 1972.

McIntyre, D., *The Coffin of St Cuthbert*, Oxford, 1950.

Shanks, C. J., *The Life and Death of St Cuthbert*, SPCK, 1987.

Webb, J. F. (trans.), *The Age of Bede* (includes the *Life of Cuthbert*), Penguin Books, 1983.

September 19th
Optional Memorial

ST THEODORE OF CANTERBURY

MY DEAREST brothers, for the love and reverence you bear our Redeemer, I beg that we may all deliberate in harmony for our Faith, preserving inviolate the decrees and definitions of our holy and respected Fathers.

– St Theodore addressing the Council of Hatfield

BORN IN 602, Theodore was a native of Tarsus in Cilicia. He had been a student in Athens and possibly Syria. Having fled the East, he became a prominent religious figure in Rome. He seems somewhat out of place in 7th-century Anglo-Saxon England. Yet this man is more than a simple curiosity, he is an example of heroic virtue as a pastor of the English Church, a sort of second Augustine sent to unite what his predecessor had founded. He is one of the most important figures in early English Christianity, both for the ecclesiastical organisation he achieved and for his promotion of learning.

It was a manifestation of the English church's loyalty and dependence upon Rome that, in 664, Wighart, the archbishop-elect of Canterbury, had journeyed to Rome to receive the Pallium at the hands of the Pope. Tragically, he died of the plague. The Holy Father Vitalian decided to appoint someone of great talent and experience to help the English peoples establish themselves more firmly in the Faith. A North African Hadrian, living in a monastery near Naples, was asked, but subsequently refused. He instead suggested Theodore as more able, agreeing to accompany him. Theodore accepted, and these two scholarly monks from diverse traditions, the remnants of the collapsing ancient world of the East, packed their scrolls in 668 to travel to British shores.

Theodore was already in his late sixties at the time of his consecration in March 668, a sage-like figure, learned and well travelled, yet hardly eager for too many new adventures, it would seem. Arriving in Canterbury in May 669, he appointed Hadrian as Abbot of Augustine's monastery of Sts Peter and Paul. Theodore soon set out for a pastoral visitation of all England, to assess the situation and appoint new bishops in vacant sees. He was able to correct much of the prevailing chaos, but he realised that the English dioceses were too large, modelled as they were on the various Kingdoms. He began to sub-divide, slowly creating greater order and stability.

He managed to unite various factions in the Church around him. Bede tells us that he was the first Archbishop to whom all England rendered obedience. He established the beginnings of a parochial system whereby towns were properly provided with churches and settled clergy. His skilful diplomacy enabled a good relationship with all the Kingdoms and obtained support and protection for the Church, beginning the process by which a unified English national and ecclesiastical identity could slowly emerge.

He called a Synod at Hertford in 673, over which he presided. He sought to implement Canon Law and establish correct discipline. The 10 canons of the Synod were based on the decrees of the Council of Chalcedon. In 680, coinciding with the third ecumenical council of Constantinople which condemned the Monothelite heresy, Theodore called a synod at Hatfield. The English bishops formally declared their support of all the holy councils of the Church, and professed their orthodoxy. Such is a testament to Theodore, who desired this purity of doctrine and unity of discipline, knowing first-hand the havoc caused by dissent and division. He was a man with a heightened sense of the Church universal.

He always promoted learning, founding with Hadrian the great Canterbury school. He set up there a remarkable classical curriculum including the study of Latin and Greek, Roman law, the rules of metre and computation. Music and medicine, in which Theodore had a particular interest, were also prominent. He introduced methods of scriptural exegesis which were almost unknown in the West. The Canterbury commentaries found in Milan in recent times reveal the prominence of the Antiochene method, more literal and historical then the Alexandrian and later Western allegorical method.

Many bishops and prominent Church leaders came from this thriving school, including St Aldhelm. Another of the school's alumni was Abbot Albinus, who encouraged Bede to write the Ecclesiastical History, sending Nothelm to Rome to research on his behalf. That England stands out almost alone in the 'dark ages' of the 8th and 9th centuries owes no small debt to the impetus given by Theodore and Hadrian.

During his 21 years in England, the country experienced what Bede saw as a 'golden age'. He was a contemporary to so many great figures: Cuthbert, Wilfrid, Chad, to name but a few. It was indeed an age of saints. It was Theodore who somehow held them all together in ecclesiastical unity. Having foretold his own death by means of a dream, he passed away on 19th September 690, at the venerable age of 88. He was laid to rest with his predecessors in the monastery church of SS Peter and Paul in Canterbury, the ruins of which can be visited today. In 1091 he was translated to a greater shrine, and in the process found to be incorrupt.

> 'Here rests the holy Primate in his tomb,
> Great Theodore, a Greek by race and name.
> A prince of pontiffs, and a blest high priest
> Who taught to all his flock the light of truth.
> The nineteenth of September was the day
> That saw his spirit burst its earthly bonds,
> Rising in rapture to a newer life
> In sweet communion with the saints on high.'
> **– Theodore's public epitaph recorded by Bede**

MPH

Places to Visit: Canterbury Cathedral is the site of his original see. The place of his original tomb can also be visited in the ruins of St Augustine's Abbey.

Further Reading:

Mayr-Harting, H., *The Coming of Christianity to Anglo-Saxon England*, Penn State Press, 1972.

Reany, W., *St Theodore of Canterbury*, St Louis, Herder, 1944.

September 24th
Memorial

OUR LADY OF WALSINGHAM

HEAVENLY Father, who from the very birth of the Church in our land, did make us the Dowry of Mary and loyal subjects of the Prince of the Apostles, grant us your Grace to continue steadfast in the Catholic Faith, ever devoted to the Virgin Mary as our Mother, and ever faithful in our allegiance to the See of Peter.

– Collect of the feast of Our Lady of Ransom

WHILST MANY liturgical celebrations of Our Lady commemorate the mysteries of the Blessed Virgin's life (such as the Immaculate Conception or the Assumption), or her appearances (the feasts of Our Lady of Lourdes or Our Lady of Fatima), the feast of Our Lady of Walsingham is one of only two feasts which celebrate her connection with a particular place. The other is the commemoration of Our Lady of Loreto (kept on 10th December in some places). But Walsingham has a certain distinction even over Loreto, in that it was by Our Lady's own request that a shrine was established to her at Walsingham. It is thus a very special feast day, of which English Catholics have every reason to feel proud.

The shrine of Our Lady at Walsingham dates from the year 1061, five years before the battle of Hastings, when Saint Edward the Confessor was King of England. The Blessed Virgin Mary appeared in a dream to the widowed lady of Walsingham, Richeldis de Faverches, and showed her the Holy House at Nazareth, in which the angel Gabriel had visited her at the annunciation. Our

Lady asked Richeldis to measure the house and to build an exact copy of it at Walsingham, in honour of the annunciation, that day which heralded our redemption. This Richeldis did, and the shrine soon attracted many pilgrims, especially after a priory of Augustinian canons was founded there in 1153. Some of the most famous pilgrims were the kings and queens of England; Edward I, Edward II and Edward III all came on pilgrimage, as did Richard II, in whose reign England first became known as 'Our Lady's Dowry'. Later still, the first Tudor monarchs also visited, Henry VII and his son Henry VIII, who is said to have walked there barefoot from nearby Earl Barsham manor. In this he followed the many thousands of ordinary pilgrims, who would leave their shoes a mile outside Walsingham at the so-called 'Slipper Chapel' (a small chapel dedicated to St Katherine of Alexandria, the patroness of pilgrims) and complete their pilgrimage barefoot. But, as we know, Henry's reverence for Our Lady's shrine was to last no longer than his adherence to the Catholic faith. After the break with Rome, the days of Walsingham were numbered. On 14th July 1538, the statue at Walsingham was taken away to the Archbishop of Canterbury's home at Lambeth Palace and afterwards destroyed. On 4th August of the same year, the Holy House built by Richeldis at Our Lady's command was destroyed as well.

Yet this was not to be the end of the shrine at Walsingham. It is likely that Catholics continued to make secret pilgrimage to the Slipper Chapel, left standing even though converted into a barn by its Protestant owners. With the 'Second Spring' for English Catholicism, which took place in the nineteenth century, the scene was set for a great revival. In 1894 Miss Charlotte Boyd started negotiations to buy the Slipper Chapel, and in the same year she was received into the Catholic Church. In 1897 work started to turn the chapel into a proper place of worship again, and on 19th August that year a new statue of Our Lady of Walsingham was placed in the Catholic Church at nearby King's Lynn. On 20th August the first pilgrimage to Walsingham in modern times took place.

From that time on, the restoration of the shrine developed rapidly. In 1931 the Anglican shrine was established in the middle of Walsingham village. In 1933 a new statue of Our Lady of Walsingham (based on the seal of the mediaeval priory) was placed in the Slipper Chapel, and on the feast of the Assumption in the same year, Bishop Youvens of Northampton celebrated the first public Mass in the chapel for four hundred years. Once again, Catholic pilgrims began to flock to Walsingham as they had done in years of old. In the Marian Year of 1954, the Apostolic Delegate crowned the statue solemnly in the presence of 15,000 people. But a still greater moment was to come when, twenty-eight years later, the statue was placed on the papal altar as His Holiness Pope John Paul II celebrated Mass in Wembley Stadium at the climax of his apostolic visit to Britain. The message of Walsingham – the joy of the annunciation and the good news of our redemption – continues to be just as relevant today as it was when Our Lady appeared to Richeldis de Faverches in a dream in 1061.

Until the new liturgical calendar for England was introduced in summer 2000, 24th September was kept as the feast of Our Lady of Ransom. This feast was especially promoted by Pope Leo XIII, who extended it to all the dioceses of England, and created himself first President of the Guild of Our Lady of Ransom, dedicated to the conversion of England. Devotion to Our Lady 'of Ransom' actually originated in Spain during the Middle Ages, when much of that country was still occupied by the Islamic Moors. In those days the devotion took the form of ransoming Christian slaves who were held by the Moors, and returning them to their homes. Pope Leo's intention in promoting this feast of Our Lady in England was that English Catholics should 'ransom' their country by their prayers and bring it back to the security of the Catholic faith. The Guild of Our Lady of Ransom, founded on 29th November 1887, was in fact closely associated with the restoration of Our Lady's shrine at Walsingham and continues to be so. Indeed, the first modern pilgrimage to Walsingham, that of 20th August 1897, was led by the Master of the Guild, Fr Philip Fletcher, alongside the parish priest of King's Lynn and the Prior of Downside. The shrine at Walsingham reminds us that England was once known as Our Lady's Dowry, and its connection with Our Lady of Ransom – now enshrined in the liturgy – reminds all English Catholics of our duty to work and pray that our country might be worthy of that title once again.

RW

Further Reading:

Walsingham: England's Nazareth, reprinted in 1990 by the Walsingham Guardians.

Bridgett, T. E., *Our Lady's Dowry*, Burns and Oates, 1875.

Gillett, M., *Walsingham and its Shrine*, Burns and Oates, 1934.

October 10th
Optional Memorial

St Paulinus

HESITATE no longer. Accept the faith and keep the commands of Him who has delivered you from all your earthly troubles.
– St Paulinus to King Edwin

'TALL OF STATURE, a little stooping, his hair black, his face ascetic, his nose slender and aquiline, his aspect both venerable and awe-inspiring'. Thus does Bede record the appearance of this early missionary. Paulinus was not part of Augustine's voyage of 597, but was sent later on a second mission from Rome in 601. The harvest of souls being so abundant, Augustine had petitioned Pope Gregory for more help. Gregory sent several of his colleagues and clergy, including Mellitus, Justus and Paulinus. For many years Paulinus lived in Kent, supporting the first mission. Yet in 625 he was consecrated bishop by Justus, Augustine's successor in Canterbury, especially for a mission of evangelisation in the north.

After Princess Ethelburga of Kent was betrothed to King Edwin of Northumbria, she journeyed north with her Christian attendants and with a bishop. This bishop was Paulinus. He came to Edwin with the princess as her spiritual counsellor and chaplain, but we are told by Bede that he had also in his mind the extension of the reign of Christ over the English peoples. There were thus two marriages over which he hoped to preside, one between King and Queen and the other between a nation and its destiny in the Divine Spouse.

Queen Ethelburga saw her husband's power increase over all the kingdoms of the English, and the slow but steady growth of the Christian faith. The King was impressed with the Christianity of Paulinus and his wife, yet was not disposed to accept it immediately. Bede tells us 'For the King was by nature a wise and prudent man, and often sat alone in silent converse with himself for long periods, turning over in his inmost heart what he should do and which religion he should follow'.

The King's near escape from an assassin's dagger and the birth of his daughter on the same Easter night of 626, were interpreted by Paulinus as providential signs. Edwin, half-convinced, vowed conversion if this God would give him victory over his enemies. But it took more than a victory over the West Saxons to convince him. While he gave up idol worship he still required much instruction from Paulinus. A letter from Pope Boniface himself as well as the ardent urgings of his wife Ethelburga were still insufficient to persuade him fully.

It took another major sign to finally persuade the king. The providential event which precipitated the conversion involved a vision which Edwin had received long ago when despairing in a prison in exile. For safety and victory over his enemies he had promised obedience to the one who would be sent to guide him in life and salvation. He would know this prophesied figure through a sign: the laying of the right hand on his head. Mysteriously, the vision was also revealed to Paulinus, and he himself fulfilled the sign one day when instructing Edwin. He approached him and laid his hand on the king's head, reviving Edwin's memory of the earlier vision and exacting the promise of obedience, 'Hesitate no longer. Accept the faith and keep the commands of Him who has delivered you from all your earthly troubles.'

At Paulinus' first exhortation to convert, Edwin, although fearful, admitted his duty with honour, but still asked for further time to convince his principal advisers and friends. Coifi, the chief priest of the pagans, admitted that the worship of the gods was ineffectual and that one should embrace sounder teachings and more effective worship. Another counsellor spoke with great wisdom, 'When we compare the present time on earth with that time of which we have no knowledge, it seems to me like the swift flight of a single sparrow through the banqueting hall where you are sitting on a winter's day with your thegns and counsellors. In the midst there is a comforting fire to warm the hall; outside the storms of winter, snow or rain raging. The sparrow flies swiftly in through one door and out through the other. While he is inside he is safe from winter storms; but after a few moments of comfort he vanishes from sight into the wintry world from which he came. Even so, man appears on earth for a while; but of what goes before or of what follows this life we know nothing. Therefore if this teaching has brought any more certain knowledge, it seems only right that we should follow it.' Edwin and his counsellors were moved by this and similar advice, and when they had heard Paulinus preach, decided to destroy the pagan idols. Coifi, mounting a horse and carrying a spear, rode to the temple of Godmundingham and cast the spear into the idols.

Thus it was on Easter Day, in the year of Our Lord 627, that Paulinus presided over the baptism of King Edwin, his noblemen and a great number of humbler folk. This took place at York, in a newly constructed wooden church dedicated to St Peter. This is the site upon which the great York Minster now stands, where so many saints and scholars would be baptised or entered into the mysteries of God down through the centuries, Oswald, Wilfrid, Egbert, Alcuin, William of York, Margaret Clitherow and Mary Ward, to mention but a few.

Bede tells us that the eagerness of the Northumbrians to accept the faith was so great that Paulinus, when accompanying the King and Queen to Yeavering, instructed and baptised without ceasing for thirty-six days. He baptised people from all the surrounding villages in the River Glen. Due to Edwin's great faith, the neighbouring province of the East Angles was introduced to the salvation of God. 'So peaceful' Bede says 'was it in those parts of Britain under King Edwin's jurisdiction that the proverb still runs true that a woman could carry her new-born babe across the island from sea to sea without any fear of harm.' At Lincoln, Edwin built a new stone church and consecrated his fellow Roman Honorius to succeed Justus at Canterbury. The new Pope, Honorius, sent a letter to Edwin encouraging him in his faith and granting the Pallium to Paulinus, creating a new ecclesiastical province for the English at York which would endure for over 1000 years.

The reign of Edwin lasted only seventeen years, with the last six dedicated to Christ. The British King Cadwalla and the Mercian King Penda slew Edwin and his army in a fierce battle at Hatfield on 12th October 633.

A dark cloud passed over the land as a great slaughter took place among the Northumbrian church and nation. Edwin's head was taken to York and subsequently placed in the church of St Peter, which he had begun to build in stone. The head was venerated as that of a saint and rested in the porch dedicated to Pope St Gregory, from whose disciples he had received the word of life.

It was Archbishop Paulinus who took Queen Ethelburga by sea back to Kent, the kingdom of her origin. They escaped with the royal children and with Edwin's best remaining guards. Paulinus brought with him the treasures of the Church in order to preserve them. Despite the traumatic experience, they were honourably received by Archbishop Honorius at Canterbury and by King Eadbald (Ethelburga's brother).

Paulinus' next mission was in Rochester, where he was made bishop and ministered until his death in October 644. He was interred at the Cathedral Church of St Andrew, in or near the sacristy. His memory was preserved there and his shrine was venerated down through the centuries.

MPH

Places to visit: York Cathedral and Rochester Cathedral which are built upon the foundations of the churches St Paulinus would have known.

Further Reading:

Gibson, E., *Northumbrian Saints*, SPCK, 1884.

Mayr-Harting, H., *The Coming of Christianity to Anglo-Saxon England*, Penn State Press, 1972.

Newman, J. H. (ed.), *Lives of the British Saints*, London, 1900.

October 12th
Optional Memorial

ST WILFRID

I HAVE made my vows to the Lord and I shall keep them, leaving, like Abraham, my kinsfolk and my father's house to visit the Apostolic See, there to learn the laws of ecclesiastical discipline so that our nation may grow in the service of God.

– The words of Wilfrid on his first pilgrimage to Rome as a young man, recorded in the *Life of Wilfrid* by Eddius Stephanus

IN TRADITIONAL Christian art, Wilfrid is aptly depicted either baptising the heathen or as a fully vested bishop with symbols of office. The first depiction points to a man who evangelised many areas of England and began the great Anglo-Saxon mission to the continent; the second indicates a figure who always upheld the traditions of the apostolic Church.

He was born in 634 to an influential Northumbrian family, and was educated at the renowned Monastery of Lindisfarne. He remained there until the age of twenty, when he conceived a great desire to go to Rome, the seat of the apostles and holy martyrs. This love for Rome and all it stood for would be the consuming passion of his life. Encouraged by Queen Elfleda and several monks, he set off. Reaching Canterbury he met up with Benet Biscop (the later founder of Wearmouth and Jarrow monasteries) who would become his travelling partner. He stopped also at Lyon, where he made the close acquaintance of Bishop Dalfinus, who treated him like a son and offered the hand of his niece to Wilfrid. Wilfrid refused this offer, explaining his deep desire to go to Rome and dedicate his life to God.

Arriving in Rome in 653, he assiduously visited the shrines of the saints and particularly the Monastery of St Andrew, from which the English mission had first begun. He was instructed by the archdeacon Boniface in the Roman discipline. On returning, he spent three years in Lyon with Bishop Dalfinus who promised to make him his successor. But Dalfinus was soon to be martyred for his faith at the hands of a local ruler; Wilfrid, although willing to follow his friend, was spared.

Wilfrid returned to Northumbria and was well received by the King. He was given land to found Ripon monastery. He was ordained priest and began to put into practice what he had learned in Rome, establishing his monastery along the lines of St Benedict's rule and Roman canon law.

In 664 at the Council of Whitby, his articulate defence of Church unity and the importance of the universal discipline won the day over the other faction which wanted ancient 'Celtic' traditions to be upheld. It was after this brilliant defence that he was asked to become a bishop. He was ordained by Agilbert at Compiegne in 665 with much grandeur, carried in Gaulish fashion by twelve bishops in a chair of gold. During Wilfrid's long absence, Chad was appointed in 666 to the diocese of Northumbria in his place. This was the beginning of all Wilfrid's problems.

On returning to England he retired to Ripon and made some missions of evangelisation, particularly to Mercia where he helped establish the Church. In 669 Archbishop Theodore, wanting a return to order, re-installed Wilfrid. Nine successful years followed. He built great churches in the Roman style at Ripon and Hexham, which could rival any in northern Europe. He implemented the Roman style of monasticism in the north, just as Augustine had done in the south, and he re-built the Church at York.

In 678, controversy struck again in a fall-out with King Egfrith, particularly over Wilfrid's part in his wife's decision to become a nun. He was banished, and set out to appeal to Rome; a very different trip from his earlier pilgrimage, yet with equal faith in the Holy See. Theodore had been persuaded by foul means against Wilfrid, and now sought to sub-divide the diocese into four. Wilfrid was supported in Rome, and, while he was there, assisted in a prestigious council at the Lateran Basilica condemning the Monothelite heresy.

On the way to Rome he had been blown off course by violent winds, and had landed on the shores of Frisia (modern-day Holland). There, throughout the winter, he had begun a great mission and converted thousands of souls. He thus initiated the great missionary work of the Anglo-Saxon Church which would flower under Willibrord and Boniface.

Unfortunately, on returning, Wilfrid failed to impress the King and was ruthlessly thrown into prison, having all his possessions confiscated. The new Queen who had stirred up much of the resentment against Wilfrid, now used his costly reliquaries for jewellery. Eventually he was sent away into exile. He went to the South Saxon people and began a mission to this hitherto neglected part of the land. He converted them and taught them many things from his vast experience, including how to fish effectively! A new monastery at Selsey was established, and a first mission to the Isle of Wight.

Again in 686 he was exonerated and called back to Northumbria, Theodore having admitted his error. He was appointed to the See of Hexham and later obtained again the See of York. The ecclesiastical situation was still very complicated, and in 691 Wilfrid entered into a fresh squabble with the new King Alfrid over endowments and boundaries. Wilfrid was banished again, this time to be protected by King Ethelred of Mercia. Here he administered large areas and, in his indomitable fashion, founded further monasteries and churches.

After an antagonistic synod held at Easterfield in 702 under the new Archbishop Bertwald, where all solicited against him, Wilfrid, for the third and final time, set out to Rome. In 703 he was supported by Pope John VI. On returning he fell ill at Meaux and was revived from death by a vision of St Michael, who told him that through the Blessed Virgin's intercession he would live a few years longer and have his possessions restored. At the Synod of the River Nidd in 705, a compromise was reached and he was given the Diocese of Hexham and the Abbey of Ripon. He relinquished York to John of Beverley.

In 709 he died at his monastery in Oundle after he had divided his treasures between the great churches of Rome, the poor, and his devoted companions (including his successor, St Acca, and his friend and later biographer, Eddius Stephanus). He was buried at Ripon. In 959, after the destruction of the Monastery, his body was moved to Canterbury and enshrined there.

St Anselm translated his relics to a greater place on 12th October, the day on which his feast was subsequently celebrated. His body is now said to lie near the memorial of Cardinal Reginald Pole, another great man of Rome.

As one of the greatest figures of the English Church's 'golden age', he has always been much celebrated. Forty-eight ancient churches were dedicated to him. His crypts at Ripon and Hexham still stand as a testament to the enduring faith for which he stood. Bede recorded for us his epitaph:

> In his long life he weathered many storms,
> Discords at home, and perils overseas.
> He ruled as bishop five and forty years,
> And passed away rejoicing to our God.
> Grant us, O Jesus, his true flock to be,
> And tread with him the road that leads to thee.

MPH

Places to visit: St Wilfrid's foundations at Ripon and Hexham, with the remarkable crypts that he built. His *sedia* is also preserved at Hexham Abbey.

Further Reading:

Kirby, D. P., *St Wilfrid of Hexham*, Oriel Press, 1974.

Mayr-Harting, H., *The Coming of Christianity to Anglo-Saxon England*, Penn State Press, 1972.

Mayr-Harting, H., *St Wilfrid*, CTS, 1986.

Webb, J. F. (trans.), *The Age of Bede* (includes the *Life of Wilfrid*), Penguin, 1983.

October 13th
Optional Memorial

ST EDWARD THE CONFESSOR

I SHALL not die but shall live. Departing from the land of the dying, I hope to see the good things of the Lord in the land of the living.

– Words of St Edward from his deathbed

Sanctus Edwardus Rex Angliæ communiter dictus CONFESSOR obijt quinto Januarij anno 1066.

MOST PEOPLE know about St Edward the Confessor because of his death in 1066, the most famous date in English history, and the succession crisis that was finally fought out on the bloody field of Hastings. In some ways this is appropriate, for the issues involved in 1066 dominated his reign – the question of succession, the threat of invasion, particularly from the Danes, and the domestic quarrels of the nobility. However, there was more to King Edward than '1066 and all that'. He faced adversity with a strong faith in providence, exercised an extraordinary piety, and was generous to the poor. Despite various potential crises, his reign was looked back upon, with the hindsight of the Norman invasion, as one of peace, prosperity and justice.

Normandy was an important factor in English politics during the tenth and eleventh centuries. Starting out as a Viking colony in north-west France, it provided refuge for the Scandinavian armies that terrorised England, and so it was crucial for English Kings to appease the Normans as far as possible. St Edward's mother, Emma, was the daughter of Count Richard I of Normandy. She married Ethelred the Unready in 1002, as part of an English attempt to neutralise Normandy, and she bore him two sons, Edward (b.1005) and Alfred. The last years of Ethelred's reign were disastrous – from 1009, large Danish armies attacked England and the two princes were driven into exile in Normandy in 1013. Here St Edward remained for nearly thirty years. Meanwhile, his father died in 1016 and Queen Emma married his supplanter, Cnut, even though he had married Aelfgifu of Northampton in 1013. At Cnut's death in 1037, it was the turn first of Harold I 'Harefoot' (1037–40), Aelfgifu's son, and then of Harthacnut (1040–42), Emma's son by Cnut. It was he who recalled his half-brother, St Edward, just before his death, probably with a view to the succession.

St Edward was crowned King of the English at Easter 1042. 'A very proper figure of a man – of outstanding height, and distinguished by his milky-white hair and beard, full face and rosy cheeks, thin white hands and long translucent fingers' – he was probably an albino. He looked every inch a king, yet his kingdom was totally unfamiliar to him. His authority was in practice checked by a handful of powerful nobles, especially Earl Godwin of Wessex, a political survivor who had retained his position under four kings in five years. In 1045, St Edward married Godwin's daughter, Edith, although Godwin was exiled in 1051 – a clear indication that St Edward was not merely 'a holy imbecile' in the hands of the nobility. Godwin returned the following year with substantial military backing, though St Edward met him in person and established acceptable terms to avoid civil war. One of Godwin's sons, Tostig, was also exiled following a rebellion in Northumberland.

The king's marriage is said to have remained unconsummated, rather like that of his contemporary, St Henry the Emperor. Whatever the motive, this led to the problem of succession. It is likely that he promised the throne to Duke William of Normandy, who seemed to be the most throne-worthy candidate, in 1051. This tied in with his pro-Norman tendencies, as seen in his appointment of Robert of Jumièges to the Sees of London and Canterbury, but infuriated many of the nobles. However, on his deathbed, St Edward supposedly appointed Earl Harold, son of Godwin, as his successor. Thus the way was paved to 1066.

Towards the end of his life, Edward was prevented from making his vowed pilgrimage to Rome. With permission from the Pope, the king instead fulfilled his vow by rebuilding St Peter's Abbey at Westminster as a vast three-hundred-feet-long Romanesque mausoleum, to which he devoted, at one time, a tenth of his income. He was too ill to attend its consecration and died shortly afterwards, on 5 January 1066. He was buried at his Abbey, where his bones remain to this day. Various legends surround his death. Several years beforehand, he had given a ring to a beggar at Westminster. Two years later a group of English pilgrims in the Holy Land met an old man, claiming to be St John the Evangelist, who gave them the ring to return to St Edward, charging them to warn him of his impending death in six months' time. The ring became his iconographic symbol.

St Edward was canonised by Alexander III in 1161, and his relics – found incorrupt in 1102 – were translated to a new shrine in Westminster Abbey on 13th October 1163, on which occasion St Aelred of Rievaulx preached. The day of his translation became his principal feast day. St Edward was called 'the Confessor' to distinguish him from his father's half-brother, King St Edward the Martyr, and he was considered a patron of England together with St Edmund, King and Martyr, until being eclipsed by St George.

St Edward was not a 'great' king in the worldly sense, and compares unfavourably to other royal saints who manifested more aptitude in government. But to see him merely as a pious puppet is to miss the point. Mgr Ronald Knox hit the nail on the head in a sermon preached in 1922: we might say, somewhat harshly, that 'when we venerate St Edward, we venerate a failure'. However, 'ask yourself which you would rather have been, in life, of all those great dead who lie in Westminster Abbey, and you will find it a difficult question to answer: there is so much that dazzles, so much that captures the imagination . . . But ask yourself which of those great dead you would rather be now, your body there, your soul far away – is there any Christian who would not ask to change places with the Confessor; who would not choose his resting-place, there to wait for the opening of the great Doomsday Book?'

NJS

Places to Visit: His intact shrine can still be visited at Westminster Abbey.

Further Reading:

Barlow, F., *Edward the Confessor*, Yale, 1998.

Bertram, J. (trans.), *Life of St Edward the Confessor by St Aelred of Rievaulx*, St Austin Press, 1997.

Newton, J. A., *Search for a Saint: Edward King*, Epworth Press, 1979.

Streeter, A., *St Edward the Confessor*, London, Catholic Truth Society.

October 26th
Optional Memorial

STS CHAD AND CEDD

LET each prepare for his own passing by vigils, prayers, and good deeds, for no man knows the hour of his death.

– St Chad to his monks before his own death

THE NORTHUMBRIAN BROTHERS Chad and Cedd, in the early part of the seventh century, were enriched and inspired by the coming of the Irish monastic tradition of Columba, to become founding fathers of Christianity in England. They both played a significant role in the Christianisation of the Anglo-Saxon peoples. From a young age, together with two other brothers, they were educated at Lindisfarne under the tutelage of Aidan and Finan.

Cedd

In 653, the newly baptised Penda, King of Mercia, asked Lindisfarne for priests to teach and baptise his people in the way of Christ. Cedd was sent, and enjoyed a period of considerable success before being recalled and sent to the land of the East Saxons, the Kingdom of Sigebert, who had only recently converted. Following his immediate success he was consecrated bishop of the long vacant See of London in 654, succeeding Mellitus who had been driven out in 610 after some early success.

Cedd brought with him a great founding era for this diocese. Churches and monasteries sprang up and vocations were plentiful from the local people. One such monastery at Ithanchester, near Bradwell-on-Sea, was built on a dilapidated Roman fortress, and due to its sturdy foundations still stands today.

King Ethelwald, knowing Cedd's success as a founder, summoned him to his native north to build a new Abbey. With his brother Cynebill, he characteristically chose a wild and lonely place on the Yorkshire moors and founded the Abbey of Lastingham. Cedd is said to have fasted for forty days before consecrating the abbey.

After playing an active role as interpreter at the Council of Whitby in 664, and after putting its decisions into practice in his own diocese despite having personal reservations about the outcome, Cedd retired to Lastingham where he died in the same year, of plague. He was first buried in open ground, but when a stone Church was erected, his relics were translated. His cult sprang up almost immediately. The Venerable Bede himself made one of the few excursions of his life to make a pilgrimage to Cedd's shrine. By the 11th century his relics were venerated with Chad's at Lichfield.

Chad

Chad succeeded his brother Cedd as Abbot of Lastingham in 664. Almost immediately he was, controversially, appointed as Bishop of Northumbria by the will of King Oswy, while the already appointed Wilfrid was away in Gaul seeking consecration. He governed the diocese with both humility and effectiveness for several years.

When the dispute over the diocese had been resolved in 669, due to the wisdom of Archbishop Theodore, Chad willingly relinquished his see and retired to Lastingham. He said at this time 'I never thought myself worthy of it, but although unworthy, I submitted out of obedience to undertake it'. He had been the unfortunate pawn played by the King of Northumbria in his dispute with Bishop Wilfrid.

Theodore, being highly impressed by Chad's obedience and humility, appointed him Bishop of the Mercians, fixing his see at Lichfield. This was a huge missionary task, one that involved continuing the earlier work of his brother Cedd. He founded a new monastery in Lincolnshire, most probably at Barrow-upon-Humber.

Chad was known to have a great devotion to the Blessed Virgin, and he consecrated a church in her honour at Lichfield. He formed a small community of seven or eight brothers to live with him around this church and to observe the monastic discipline. Bede tells us that, 'He administered his diocese in great holiness of life, following the example of the ancient fathers'.

In the typical simplicity of a Lindisfarne monk, he would journey around his vast diocese on foot, in order to be a better apostolic witness, a servant like unto Christ. There is a wonderful account in Bede's *Ecclesiastical History* that describes how Theodore, on his own pastoral visitation of the different churches, told Chad that he must be a practical and effective bishop, as well as humble and simple. He lifted the diminutive Chad onto a horse so that he could travel more freely, and uphold the dignity of his office.

After just two years we are informed that he received an angelic visitation, which told him of his approaching death by plague. He calmly summoned his brethren about him and addressed them, 'Return to the Church, and speak to the brethren that they in their prayers recommend my passage to the Lord, and that they may be careful to provide for their own, the whereof is uncertain, by watching, prayer and good works.'

He died on 2nd March, 672, and was buried in his own Church of St Mary, but was soon translated to the cathedral church of St Peter. Bede gives us a description of his shrine, at which many miracles took place and to which many pilgrimages were made. His relics were preserved at the reformation by recusants and are now venerated in the Catholic Cathedral of St Chad in Birmingham (they were recently verified as authentic by scientific tests). A copy of an illuminated Mercian Gospel Book associated with Chad is still preserved at Litchfield cathedral library.

MPH

Places to Visit:

Cedd – The ruins of his foundations at Ithanchester and Lastingham can be visited. It is worth recalling upon a visit to St Paul's in London that this was the site of the original cathedral of the East Saxons where Cedd was bishop.

Chad – The Catholic Cathedral of Birmingham enshrines the authentic relics of St Chad. A visit to his original foundation and shrine at Lichfield is essential.

Further Reading:

Austerberry, J., *Chad: Bishop and Saint*, Derby, English Life Publications, 1984.

Gibson, E., *Lives of the Northumbrian Saints*, SPCK, 1884.

Mayr-Harting, H., *The Coming of Christianity to Anglo-Saxon England*, Penn State Press, 1972.

November 3rd
Optional Memorial

ST WINEFRIDE

AS SURE as what is most sure,
sure as that spring primroses
shall new-dapple next year,
sure as to-morrow morning,
amongst come-back-again things,
things with a revival,
things with a recovery,
Thy name [Winefride shall live]

– From *St Winefride's Well*
by Gerard Manley Hopkins
(1844–1889)

DESPITE THE ANGLO-SAXON invasion, there survived, particularly in the western areas of the isle, a vibrant and early form of Christianity that had been adopted by the original British people. There are many saints from this western British church, from before, during, and after the coming of the Gregorian mission, who have an identity all of their own. Winefride represents for us the later part of this rich tradition.

Her cult defies evaluation through purely technical tools. The earliest written life of her comes in the 12th century, written at Shrewsbury by a prior Robert, at the time of the translation of her sacred relics in 1138. This is some five hundred years after her own time. While this popular account has no doubt been embroidered, we have in our hands a very popular 500-year cultic tradition. The reality of her personage and the basic facts of her life are easily acknowledged, while certain details of the later written accounts are disputed. Her cult is indeed bigger than history. Whether or not the 12th-century story correctly represents the reality of the 7th-century saint cannot be proved by the limited means of historical methodology.

There are slight deviations in the traditions surrounding her life, yet certain common features are clear. She was born of a noble family in the town of Holywell (or Trefyno, in Flintshire) and she was connected as niece (or close blood relation) to St Beuno, who had founded a church in that settlement. Her father, Therith, was a British nobleman.

She had an early attraction to the things of God, and apparently sought the consecrated life of virginity. Yet she was pursued by courtiers, particularly Caradoc, the son of a neighbouring prince from Hawarden. He is to become the great villain of the story in attempting to seduce her. She refused, and tried to flee to the church of her uncle, but he pursued her and in frustration struck off her head. A fountain sprang up where her head hit the ground, a feat akin to the tradition surrounding the martyrdom of the Apostle Paul at Tre Fontane in Rome. St Beuno, repositioning her head, raised her from the dead in a miracle not unknown to the Holy Apostles of Christ throughout the history of the Church, and one common in Celtic hagiography. We are told that the white scar remained where the neck had been originally cut. Her original name had been Brewa, but was later rendered Winefride, 'Wen' in old British signifying 'White', thus referring either to her purity of heart or to the white scar around her neck.

These were the dramatic events upon which the whole Winefride tradition developed. It was from the holy well, formed from the crashing of her head to the ground, that medieval pilgrims focused their attention, and sought the intercession of this holy virgin. It is this site that is still in Catholic hands, and can be visited today.

She seems to have first lived the consecrated life of a nun under the guidance of St Beuno in or around Holywell. (There are some variations in the tradition about her exact movements, yet we know monastic institutions of the region had some inter-connection which would easily account for this). After Beuno departed for the Monastery of Clynnog Fawr, she eventually came to settle at the community at Gwytherin. Here, under the direction of a certain St Eleris, she spent her time in the solitude of a remote mountain valley. Eventually she became abbess and ended her life in great holiness.

Her relics were venerated down through the centuries, as well as her shrine at Holywell. The cult seems to have been limited in the early middle ages to North Wales and the Marches. In 1138 her relics were translated to Shrewsbury. It was from this time, and the writing of the first life by Prior Robert of Shrewsbury, that devotion to her spread far and wide. In 1391, Thomas Arundel, Archbishop of Canterbury, ordered the festival to be observed throughout his province. Archbishop Chichele of St David's in 1415, having particular interest in the Welsh saints, raised her feast to a higher rank. Holywell and Saint David's were to become the most important shrines in Wales. Most notably, in 1416 Henry V made the pilgrimage on foot from Shrewsbury to Holywell (Edward IV is said to have done the same). The fine chapel still standing at Holywell was erected by Lady Margaret Beaufort, mother of Henry VII, after the battle of Bosworth Field in 1485. This attests to the importance of this shrine and the cult of Winefride. Pilgrimage remarkably continued throughout the reformation period, with many cures reported at the spring. In 1629 it is reported that fourteen thousand pilgrims visited. It became an important recusant centre and a hiding place for priests. An inscription 'IHS 1687' on the side of the well marks the occasion when King James II and Queen Mary of Modena made a pilgrimage. In 1774, Dr. Johnson saw people bathing there. It is the best preserved medieval pilgrimage centre of its kind in Britain today, with its medieval architectural complex and well.

MPH

Places to Visit: The shrine complex at Holywell

Further Reading:

Chadwick, N., *The Age of the Saints in the Early Celtic Church*, Lanerch, 1960.

Charles-Edwards, T., *St Winefride and her Well*, CTS, 1971.

David, C., *St Winefride's Well – A History and Guide*, Holywell, 1971.

Doble, G. H., *The Lives of the Welsh Saints*, University of Wales Press, 1991.

Swift, T., *The Life of St Winefride*, Holywell, 1906.

November 7th
Optional Memorial

St Willibrord

HE WAS of a becoming stature, venerable in his aspect, comely in his person, graceful, and always cheerful in his speech and countenance, wise in his counsel, unwearied in preaching and all apostolic functions, amidst which he was careful to nourish the interior life of his soul by assiduous prayer, singing of psalms, watching, and fasting.

– A description of St Willibrord by his biographer Alcuin

THE LIFE of St Willibrord is one which exemplifies the virtues of patience and resignation to the will of God. It was his unhappy fate to see much of his life's work swept away after years of missionary labour, yet he never became daunted. He continued to work tirelessly in his task of preaching the Gospel, and trusted in the providence of God to make all things well in the end.

Willibrord was born in Northumbria around 658, and studied first at Ripon under the guidance of St Wilfrid, and then for twelve years in Ireland at the abbey of Rathmelsig under Sts Egbert and Wigbert. After this he was ordained a priest. Around the year 690 he set off with twelve companions to the heathen countries of Frisia, or Friesland, in what is now modern Holland, and preached the faith of Christ there with great success.

In 693 he visited Rome to obtain the Pope's approval for his work, and he paid a return visit there in 695. This time he was consecrated Archbishop of the Frisians, with his See established at Utrecht. At this time Willibrord received much practical help from the ruler of the Franks, Pepin of Heristal, and the work of evangelisation went forward vigorously. Missionaries were sent into Denmark and Upper Friesland, and the great monastery of Echternach was founded in what we today call Luxembourg, becoming the spiritual centre of all this missionary activity. At the same time the work was often difficult and dangerous. It is recorded that Willibrord himself was once nearly killed by an outraged mob of pagans, after he cut down a tree which they held sacred and used for their heathen rituals.

Things became more difficult still after 714, when Pepin of Heristal died and was succeeded by Duke Radbod. Radbod was a pagan Frisian who hated everything to do with the Franks, including Christianity. He had refused baptism, saying, 'I prefer to be with my ancestors in hell than with a few beggars in heaven'. Unsurprisingly, therefore, his reign did enormous damage to the Christian cause, and Willibrord was forced to watch the destruction of almost all the fruits of his missionary endeavours. Yet patience won the day. After five years Radbod died, and under his successors the missionaries were free to begin their work again, venturing as far afield as Denmark and Thuringia. This time Willibrord had the help of St Boniface, whose zeal impressed him enormously.

Towards the end of his life, Willibrord hoped that Boniface would succeed him as Archbishop of Utrecht, and so safeguard all the good that had been achieved. Yet once again he was doomed to disappointment. Boniface revealed that he had made a solemn promise to God to work as an evangelist among the heathen, and begged not to be forced to take on the cares of a diocese. Willibrord, who had worked so long as a missionary himself, understood the younger man's concerns and so did not press his case. 'Willibrord, the man of God, when he learned of the saint's great promise, bestowed on him a benediction, and immediately gave him liberty to go away.' (*The Life of St Boniface*).

Willibrord died, full of years and good works, at Echternach, the monastery he had founded, whilst on retreat. It was 7th November 739. On Whit Tuesday each year, an ancient celebration still takes place in honour of St Willibrord. Through the streets of Echternach and around the saint's tomb, dancing pilgrims and brass bands process in homage to their heavenly patron, keeping alive the memory of the saint in medieval fashion.

RW

Places to Visit: The Catholic shrine of St Willibrord at Echternach, Luxembourg

Further Reading:

Grieve, A., *Willibrord, Missionary in the Netherlands 691–739*, Westminster, The Society for the Propagation of the Gospel in Foreign Parts, 1923.

Huelin, G., *Saint Willibrord and his Society*, Faith Press, 1960.

Meyrick, T., *Life of Saint Willibrord, Archbishop of Utrecht and Apostle of Holland*, Burns and Oates, 1877.

Talbot, C. H. (trans. & ed.), *The Anglo-Saxon Missionaries in Germany*, London, Sheed and Ward, 1954.

November 16th
Optional Memorial

St Edmund of Abingdon

IT IS you, Lord, in whom I have believed, whom I have loved, about whom I have preached and taught. You are my witness that I have sought nothing else but you.

– St Edmund from his deathbed

EDMUND WAS BORN about 1175 into a merchant family in Abingdon, where a chapel now marks the place of his birth. As proof of the spiritual pedigree of this saint, it is known that his father later became a monk and his mother was renowned for particular holiness. From simple beginnings he was to become the spiritual primate of the country, a testimony to the elasticity of medieval society.

After leaving the Abbey school of Abingdon with its memories of the great St Erconwold, he entered the new university scene at Oxford and then Paris. Between 1195 and 1201 he tutored in Oxford, before again returning to Paris to study theology, queen of the sciences and the pinnacle of the scholastic curriculum. It was here in this thriving yet worldly city, amongst the doctors of the Church, that he wrote his *Moralities on the Psalms*.

During his early years at Oxford he had consecrated his virginity to the Blessed Virgin Mary by placing a ring on her statue's finger. When the ring became stuck he took this as a sign that Mary had accepted his offer and indeed had become his spouse. Matthew Paris, Edmund's biographer, tells us that this was confirmed some time later when he was walking in the meadows of Oxford. Our Lord appeared to him 'shining with great clarity' and said 'I am Jesus Christ, the son of Blessed Mary the Virgin, your spouse, whom you wedded with a ring and took as your Lady. I know the secrets of your heart and I have been your inseparable companion as you walked alone. From now on I promise that I and my Mother, your spouse, shall be your helpers and comforters.'

Returning to Oxford after 1214, he became a great pioneer of the new scholasticism. He wrote many important biblical commentaries. In his scriptural exegesis he promoted a healthy balance between a spiritual/mystical reading and a more literal/historical one. His most famous work was a spiritual treatise called *Speculum Ecclesiae* ('The Mirror of the Church'). He always stressed the importance of the inner life and mental prayer, especially on the humanity of Christ and his passion. He developed the devotion of gazing upon the five wounds of Christ and repeating the invocation, 'We adore thee, O Christ'. He would say, 'I would rather repeat five words with my heart, than five thousand which my soul does not relish with affection and understanding'. He was known during these years to have advanced in the path of mystical contemplation. He was Oxford's first master to become a saint, and St Edmund Hall takes its name from him. The crypt and chancel of the ancient Church of St Peter-in-the-East were probably built by Edmund while he lived there.

After a short spell as Treasurer at Salisbury Cathedral, he was appointed Archbishop of Canterbury in 1233, a role in which he particularly excelled. His reforms were widespread and effective. He gathered around him a group of outstanding individuals, including his friend and former pupil Richard Wiche (later St Richard of Chichester). In 1234–6, a civil war between the barons of the Welsh Marches and Henry III was averted owing to Edmund's intervention. Like so many of his saintly predecessors, he had to fight vigorously to defend the freedom of the Church. Despite being a diplomat, his role was unavoidably controversial. In 1240, already worn out by his labours, he had to flee from the country in order to appeal to the Pope against the harassment of Henry III over the position of Church law in the realm.

Into this virtual exile he was accompanied by his friend Richard, who supported him at Soissy in Burgundy when his health failed, and tended him as death approached. An observer records 'Each leaned upon the other; saint upon saint; master upon disciple and disciple upon master'. From his deathbed, Edmund prayed, 'It is you, Lord, in whom I have believed, whom I have loved, about whom I have preached and taught. You are my witness that I have sought nothing else but you.'

After passing from this world on 16th November 1240, he was buried in the Cistercian Abbey at Pontigny and canonised just six years later. Surprisingly, he was never translated back to England. His flock would now have to come to him, including Henry III on a pilgrimage of repentance. Seven years after his death, in the presence of King St Louis and Queen Blanche, the body of Edmund was disinterred only to be found whole and entire. This was re-confirmed in the 17th century, when the relics were again inspected. Escaping the iconoclasm of the Reformation, his shrine remains in France to this day.

MPH

Places to Visit: His shrine can be found at the Cistercian Abbey of Pontigny

Further Reading:

Lawrence, C. H., *St Edmund of Abingdon: A Study in Hagiography and History*, Oxford University Press, 1960.

Lawrence, C. T. (trans.), *The Life of St Edmund by Matthew Paris*, London, Sandpiper Books, 1996.

Newbolt, M. R., *Edmund Rich, Archbishop and Saint*, London, SPCK, 1928.

de Paravicini, F., *Life of St Edmund of Abingdon, Archbishop of Canterbury*, Burns and Oates, 1898.

November 16th
Optional Memorial

St Margaret of Scotland

SO only he eats and drinks judgment to himself, who without confession and penance, and with the defilement of his sins, presumes to draw near to the sacred mysteries. But we who have confessed our faults, on the day of the Lord's resurrection receive the body and blood of the Immaculate Lamb not to judgment, but to remission of sins and the salutary preparation of our souls for eternal blessedness.

– St Margaret's only recorded words

IT IS NOT ONLY out of respect for the Scots that their holy queen and patron is included in the revised calendar for England; St Margaret is a cosmopolitan figure. She was born in England in 1046 with an impressive English pedigree – grand-daughter of King Edmund II Ironside and daughter of Edward the Exile, who had been forced abroad after England's submission to Cnut in 1016. St Margaret was brought up in exile, receiving most of her education in far-away Hungary. The Normans conquered her native England when she was 20, and the princess took refuge at the Scottish court – a sensible move, for, as a close relative of St Edward the Confessor and sister of Edgar the Atheling, briefly proclaimed king in 1066 and involved in the anti-Norman revolts of 1069–70, she was in considerable personal danger. However, this period of uncertainty and fear had a happy ending, for she fell in love with the king, Malcolm III Canmore, and they married in 1069.

The new Queen of Scots had a remarkable impact on Scotland. It was a time of Anglicisation at the Scots court – as can be seen in the peculiarly un-Scottish names given to her children (Edgar, Edward, Matilda . . .) – as well as Church reform, of which she became a notable patron. She revived the abbey of Iona, once the home of St Columba and St Aidan, and founded Dunfermline Abbey, which became the burial place of the Scottish royal family. She became known as the 'Pearl of Scotland', partly owing to the fact that her name is derived from the Greek 'margaron', meaning pearl.

In her personal life, St Margaret was devout and austere, eating little, observing the penitential seasons with great rigour and rising at midnight to recite Matins, sometimes with the king. She also spent much time giving alms, freeing English prisoners-of-war (not surprising, given her English background) and producing beautiful ecclesiastical needlework for the greater glory of God.

The most charming aspect of St Margaret is her happy marriage to King Malcolm. Her great zeal for the Faith obviously affected her husband for, as one early biographer wrote, 'what she rejected, he rejected . . . what she loved, he, for love of her, loved too' for he saw that 'Christ truly dwelt in her heart'. The royal couple was blessed with six sons and two daughters, including Matilda, who married Henry I of England and was popularly known as 'Good Queen Maud'. It is through her that the present Royal Family can trace its descent from the Saxon kings. Two of her sons became kings of Scotland – Alexander I and David, himself venerated as a saint and one of Scotland's greatest rulers. It is in this regard that she is considered a patron of motherhood.

St Margaret's life ended as it had begun – with a background of great uncertainty and personal sadness. She was already on her deathbed when Malcolm and one of her sons, Edward, were killed in battle against the forces of William Rufus. She died four days later and was buried with her husband at Dunfermline, although her body was moved to a new shrine at her canonisation in 1250. She was moved again at the Reformation – not to an anonymous grave like many other saints, but to the splendour of a specially built chapel in the Escorial, Madrid. Her head meanwhile found its way to the English Jesuit house in Douai, and in 1673 she was named patron of Scotland.

NJS

Places to Visit: Her former Catholic shrine (the relics have all been lost) can be visited at the Escorial, Madrid, as can her original resting place at Dunfermline.

Further Reading:

Menzies, L. (ed.), *St Margaret Queen of Scotland and Her Chapel*, St Margaret's Chapel Guild, 1972.

Wilson, A. J., *St Margaret, Queen of Scotland*, Edinburgh, John Donald, 2001.

November 17th
Optional Memorial

ST HILDA

ALL who knew her called her 'Mother', such were her wonderful godliness and grace.
– St Bede writing about St Hilda

TRADITION HAS IT that, while St Hilda's mother was pregnant, she dreamt that she found a precious jewel under her garments which 'emitted such a brilliant light that all Britain was lit by its splendour'. And, indeed, her daughter, as the future Abbess of Whitby, would fit this description very well. A highly capable and intelligent monastic leader, she is an effective tonic to those who write off the involvement of women in the early English church – at the highest level, in St Hilda's case – just as she proves herself to be an inspiring role-model for today's women.

St Hilda's life is neatly divided into two halves, each lasting 33 years. We know little about the first half, which covers the period leading up to her decision to enter the monastic life. She was born in 614 into the extended royal family of Northumbria, at that time still pagan, although she was converted and baptised at the age of 13 by St Paulinus, the celebrated apostle of York, together with her great-uncle, King St Edwin, and his household. For the next 20 years she lived a secular life, probably in and around the court. Given her comparatively late entry into the religious life and the fact that our main source, St Bede, never calls her a 'virgin', it is quite likely that she was married, although there is no mention of her having had children.

Her life was radically changed at the age of 33, when, with the encouragement of St Aidan, she decided to dedicate the remainder of her life to God. Originally she planned to set off for Gaul, where her sister, St Hereswitha, was a nun at Chelles. Saxon sanctity seems to have run in the family for, before taking the veil, St Hereswitha had mothered three saints: Sts Sexburga, Withburga and Ethelburga. However, St Hilda never did cross the Channel. St Aidan arranged for her to live the monastic life with some companions in Northumbria, and she soon found herself appointed Abbess of a monastery at Hartlepool, founded by one Heiu, a 'devout servant of Christ'. The reputation of the new abbess and her community grew, and in 655 King Oswy's young daughter, St Elfeda (or Aelfraed), was given to the convent as a thanksgiving for her father's recent victory over the pagan Penda at Winwaed (654).

The community at Hartlepool was soon on the move. In 657 St Hilda founded the great double monastery of Streonaeshalch, later known as Whitby, which quickly became famous as a centre of learning. It produced five future bishops, as well as St Caedmon, a cowherd who discovered a gift for poetry and is remembered as one of our first vernacular poets. Moreover, as a 'royal' abbey, Whitby became the mausoleum of the Northumbrian kings. Such was its importance to Anglo-Saxon Christianity that a famous Synod was held there in 664 which, amongst other things, resolved the dispute between the Celtic and Roman 'parties' over the dating of Easter. This complex conflict had led to many awkward situations: for example, at the Northumbrian court, Celtic-trained King Oswy found himself celebrating Easter when his queen, Roman-trained St Enfleda, was still observing Lent! But the crux of the matter went beyond such liturgical niceties to the whole question of how much influence Rome should have over the English Church. This synod, resulting in the victory of the Roman side under St Wilfrid, was hosted by Abbess Hilda. Bede mentions her as a sympathiser of the Celtic 'party', although she happily abided with the decisions of the synod. The fact that Bede bothers even to mention her opinions on the matter shows her considerable prestige as a royal abbess, a woman of deep learning and wisdom, and an adviser of both princes and paupers.

Her last six years were marked by severe illness, though she continued zealously to guide her double community of monks and nuns. She died in 680, to be succeeded by St Elfleda, who ruled with her widowed mother, the former Queen, St Enfleda. Whitby's glorious days were, however, numbered. The abbey was sacked by the Danes in around 867, although it would be re-founded in the late eleventh century.

St Hilda's holiness did indeed light Britain by its splendour. Her name already appears in the early eighth-century Calendar of St Willibrord, and fifteen medieval churches were dedicated to her. Her shrine attracted many pilgrims, even though both Glastonbury and Gloucester claimed her relics – itself admirable testimony to her popularity.

NJS

Places to Visit: The spectacular ruins of her Monastery at Whitby can be easily visited.

Further Reading:

Hume, B., *Footprints of the Northern Saints*, DLT, 1996.

Ellison, C., *St Hilda of Whitby*, Catholic Printing Company, 1964.

Mayr-Harting, H., *The Coming of Christianity to Anglo-Saxon England*, Penn State Press, 1972.

Mundahl-Harris, S., *St Hilda and Her Times*, 1980.

November 17th
Optional Memorial

St Hugh of Lincoln

EAT well, drink well and serve God well.
– A maxim of St Hugh

HUGH OF LINCOLN, the first Carthusian monk to be canonised, was born at Avalon in Burgundy c.1140. At the age of eight his mother died, leaving Hugh and his father, both of whom joined the Augustinian community at Villarbenoît, near Grenoble. This religious order seems to have suited Hugh's father more than himself, for, at the age of twenty-five, Hugh left the Augustinian Canons to join the Carthusian community at the Grande Chartreuse.

As a Carthusian, Hugh lived his life between his cell and the church. His cell, says William of St Thierry, was a womb; there a monk was 'cherished, nourished and enfolded' so that he might be led 'to the fullness of perfection'. The monks lived in cells arranged around a large cloister. Further down the mountain on which the Grande Chartreuse was situated, lived the lay brothers who were answerable to a monk named the procurator. Some ten years or so after Hugh's admission to the Chartreuse, he was given this office, an appointment that would prepare him well for his life as a bishop. The Rule reminded the procurator that he must never neglect the inner life, seizing every available spare moment to offer up prayer and praise to Almighty God. According to his biographer, Adam of Eynsham, Hugh embraced a life which 'encouraged solitude not isolation; the monks had separate cells but their hearts were united. Each of them lived apart . . . but did not live for himself.'

Soon after becoming procurator, Hugh was invited by King Henry II to become prior of his struggling Charterhouse at Witham in Somerset. This community had been founded in reparation for the murder of St Thomas of Canterbury, but had not been well endowed and had previously been ruled by two unsuitable priors in succession. Under Hugh, the Charterhouse flourished, attracting many fine new monks.

In 1186 King Henry wished to appoint Hugh as Bishop of Lincoln, England's largest see. At first Hugh declined, finally accepting it only in obedience to the Prior of the Grande Chartreuse. As bishop he revived the diocese, appointing new canons, refounding the academic work of the Lincoln schools, extending the cathedral and ceaselessly travelling throughout his diocese consecrating churches, confirming and carrying out visitations. Three popes made Hugh judge-delegate for some of the most important cases of his time, and all the while he tended the sick and indeed risked his life in riots to save some Jews from almost certain death.

All Hugh's activity, however, was deeply rooted in his solid Carthusian manner of living; his hairshirt, his refusal to eat meat and his regular Saturday confessions all bear testimony to a life deeply imbued with Carthusian spirituality. Yet this fundamental spirituality proved itself in its adaptability to his new circumstances upon being consecrated bishop. As a bishop, Hugh was known to keep a good table for his guests, he continued to build a splendid cathedral for the worship of God, he was renowned for his witty conversation, all in all embodying one of his maxims, 'Eat well, drink well and serve God well'.

Hugh had a passionate concern for the souls of the dead, sometimes going to great lengths to ensure that all men and women had a decent Christian burial. He himself died on 16th November 1200, in London, after having visited various French monasteries and witnessed the signing of an important treaty. He died while the Nunc Dimittis was being sung, dressed as a Carthusian, wearing his hairshirt and a monastic habit, and lying on a bed of ashes. His funeral cortege arrived in Lincoln on Thursday 23rd November, whereupon the kings of England and Scotland, John Lackland and William the Lion, helped to carry his coffin. Swiftly many miracles were attributed to his intercession, so that, after due investigation, Cardinal Stephen Langton announced Hugh's canonisation by Pope Honorius III.

Among the sayings of St Hugh which have survived, one in particular suggests the pastoral love which fired Hugh's heart and so endeared him to his people: whoever practised charity in his heart, truth on his lips, and chastity in the body, he said, would have a reward in heaven equal to that of monks and nuns. The clear message is that every Christian is called to be holy in his or her own distinctive way.

GS

Places to Visit: His original shrine and cathedral can be visited in Lincoln.

Further Reading:

Farmer, D. H., *Saint Hugh of Lincoln*, London, Darton, Longman & Todd, 1985.

Forbes, F. A, *St Hugh of Lincoln*, Washbourne, 1917.

Garton, C. (trans.), *The Metrical Life of Saint Hugh of Lincoln*, Lincoln, Honeywood Press, 1986.

Mayr-Harting, H. (ed.), *Saint Hugh of Lincoln: Lectures delivered at Oxford and Lincoln to celebrate the eighth centenary of St Hugh's consecration as Bishop of Lincoln*, Oxford, Clarendon Press, 1987.

November 30th
Feast

St Andrew

HAIL, precious cross, that hast been consecrated by the body of my Lord, and adorned with his limbs as with rich jewels. I come to thee exulting and glad: receive me with joy into thy arms.

– The words that St Andrew spoke, according to tradition, when seeing his cross

ST ANDREW is known in the East as *Protocletus* because he was the first to be called by the Lord. Born at Bethsaida, the son of Jonah and the brother of Simon, he was a fisherman by trade, working at Capernaum. At first he was a disciple of the Baptist, and was with him when he saw Jesus pass by and exclaimed 'Behold, the Lamb of God' (Jn 1:36). St Andrew wanted to know more. He went after Jesus and asked Him where He dwelt – 'Come and see' was the reply. Soon afterwards, he brought his brother Simon to Jesus, who renamed him 'Peter'. Bede thus referred to him as the 'Introducer to Christ'. Jesus called them both to discipleship with the famous words, 'Come, follow me, and I will make you fishers of men'. They left their nets at once. The

Gospels single out St Andrew for his role in the feeding of the five thousand and in the episode of the Greeks who wanted to meet Jesus.

After Pentecost, St Andrew travelled widely, spreading the Gospel to different peoples. Traditionally, he started these missionary journeys with St Peter, before they parted their ways. St Andrew is symbolically seen as an 'Apostle of the East' whilst his brother, journeying towards Rome, became an 'Apostle of the West'. Concentrating his efforts in Asia Minor, southern Russia and Greece, Andrew is said to have consecrated the first bishops of Byzantium and of Kiev. At Patros (modern Patrai), in southern Greece, he infuriated the Proconsul, Aegeates, by converting members of his family, including his brother, Stratoklis, who became the first bishop of Patros. The Proconsul ordered Andrew's arrest, scourging and crucifixion on an 'X-shaped' cross (*crux decussata*).

It has been suggested that he was crucified on a traditionally-shaped cross, like his Master, and that the idea of the 'X' shape came from the way the relic kept at St Victor, near Marseilles, was displayed. It is said that, upon seeing the cross at a distance, he cried out: 'Hail, precious cross, that hast been consecrated by the body of my Lord, and adorned with his limbs as with rich jewels. I come to thee exulting and glad: receive me with joy into thy arms'. St Andrew is thus called the 'Apostle of the Cross'. He remained on the cross two or three days, teaching the multitudes, before giving his soul to God and thus, as St Paulinus puts it, confirming the faith which he had preached by his blood. Aegeates supposedly committed suicide when he realised what he had done, and St Andrew was buried at Patros.

The man traditionally held responsible for the cult of St Andrew in Scotland was a fourth-century Abbot of Patros, St Regulus or Rule. Around the time of the Emperor Constantine's removal of the apostle's relics to Constantinople in 357, he was commanded by an angel in a dream to keep a part of the body – an arm, kneecap, tooth and a couple of fingers – and take them to an unknown destination at 'the ends of the earth'. Reaching the coast of Scotland, he was told to build a church in Fife to house the bones – the origin of St Andrews. Many believe that it was actually Bishop Acca of Hexham, a relic collector par excellence, who brought the relics to Scotland in 733. Whatever the origins of the relics, St Andrews soon became the religious capital of Scotland and a major centre of pilgrimage.

By the Middle Ages, St Andrew was considered the Patron of Scotland, and his diagonal cross used as a national emblem perhaps as early as the

Scots' victory over Athelstan of Wessex in the tenth century. The Chapel of Relics at St Andrews was destroyed by a mob on 14th June 1559, but the Catholic Cathedral in Edinburgh, home of the National Shrine, contains two relics of the apostle. The Marquess of Bute gave one, originating from Amalfi, to Archbishop Strain in 1879; the other was presented to Cardinal Gray by Paul VI upon his elevation to the College of Cardinals in 1969, with the words, 'St Peter gives you his brother'.

St Andrew's position as Patron of Scotland survived the religious changes of the sixteenth century, and his feast is still a great day for typically Scottish celebrations. In honour of the saint, James VII of Scotland (II of England) established the 'Order of St Andrew' or the 'Most Ancient Order of the Thistle', consisting of the monarch and sixteen members.

The rest of the apostle's remains were kept at Constantinople until they were moved to Italy (the body to Amalfi, the head to Rome) after the fall of that great city in 1204. Pope Paul VI returned the head of St Andrew, which had been presented to Pius II in 1461 and treasured at St Peter's, to Constantinople. St Andrew is patron of Greece, Russia and Scotland, as well as of fishermen. He is also invoked against the gout and stiff necks.

NJS

Places to Visit: St Andrew's Church in Amalfi, Italy; Constantinople (modern Istanbul); as well as the many places in the Holy Land connected to his life.

December 29th
Optional Memorial

St Thomas Becket

I KNOW your plans for the Church; you will assert claims which I, if I were archbishop, must needs oppose.
– St Thomas to King Henry

HE WAS BORN about 1117 in the City of London, near Cheapside, only twenty yards from where, several centuries later, another martyr would be born, his namesake St Thomas More. He was educated at Merton Priory in Surrey, and later at Paris. On his return to England he entered the household of Theobald, Archbishop of Canterbury. Here his obvious talents made a great impression, and Theobald soon made him Archdeacon of Canterbury. Before long, Thomas had acquired not only ecclesiastical but political prestige. In 1154, at Theobald's recommendation, King Henry II made him

Chancellor of England, one of the most important positions in the land. He soon became the king's trusted confidant and friend, and he enjoyed the situation to the full. He flaunted his wealth and status whenever possible, and even appeared at the siege of Toulouse in full armour, which for a cleric was unusual to say the least. Despite these displays of prestige and power, Thomas was not without virtue in these early days. Amidst King Henry's corrupt and immoral court he stood out for his personal honesty and chastity. It was not a great surprise to anyone when, after the death of Theobald in 1161, the king selected Thomas to succeed him as Archbishop of Canterbury. He was consecrated in 1162.

Almost immediately, Thomas' friendship with Henry came to a bitter end. The King had hoped that the new archbishop would continue to serve as Chancellor, and assist him in his campaign to extend royal control over the Church. Thomas, however, who knew what his new responsibility demanded of him, resigned the post of Chancellor and became instead a staunch defender of the Church's rights. It was a time of great conflict between Church and State. King Henry was trying to reassert the rights of the crown, forfeited during the civil war which had raged during the reign of his predecessor, Stephen. While his efforts were partly directed at the powerful barons, they were also aimed at the Church. With Thomas, Henry's dispute ostensibly centred around the so-called 'criminous clerks', clerics who committed crimes. Under medieval canon law, which was also reflected in civil law, a cleric could only be tried in special ecclesiastical courts, where the sentences were much more lenient than in the secular courts. Henry wanted to abolish this privilege and have equal justice for all, which Thomas opposed. Yet the King's real ambitions went much further. He wished to make the Church completely the servant of the State, and the issue of the 'criminous clerks' was only a part of this agenda, as subsequent events would show.

In 1163, at Council in Westminster, King Henry demanded that the bishops submit to 'the ancient customs' of England. A year later, at Clarendon in Wiltshire, he had these customs put into writing, the so-called 'Constitutions of Clarendon'. There were sixteen of these and they revealed the king's real motives clearly. The fourth, for instance, forbade any cleric to leave England without the king's permission. The eighteenth forbade any appeals to Rome without the king's consent. It was now clear that the freedom of the Church was at stake. Thomas, who had at first agreed to accept the 'customs', now refused, and Pope Alexander III subsequently supported this refusal. Henry was furious and, by way of revenge, began proceedings against the archbishop for crimes he had supposedly committed while in office as Chancellor. Thomas refused to accept the legality of such a show-trial and fled to Pontigny in France, where he remained in exile until 1170, studying canon law and living a life of penance.

Attempts to bring about a reconciliation with the king achieved nothing, until, in June 1170, Henry committed a grave mistake. He had his son, the young Henry, crowned joint king to reign alongside him. The coronation was carried out by the Archbishop of York, one of Thomas Becket's enemies. This action was in total defiance of the rights of the Archbishop of Canterbury, whose privilege it was always to carry out coronations. Moreover, it involved outright disobedience to the pope, who had explicitly forbidden the northern bishops to take part in such a ceremony. It provided the final proof that Henry's real intention was to subject the Church to his own convenience. The bishops involved were excommunicated and the king threatened with severe penalties. Faced with this turn of events, Henry had no alternative but to retreat, and on 22nd July 1170, at Freteval in France, a compromise was reached which was very favourable to Thomas. He made a triumphant return to England, but first reaffirmed the excommunication of the disobedient bishops.

This last action sent King Henry into a fury. Still in France, he said things which caused four knights to cross to England seeking Thomas' life. On 29th December the end came. The four knights sought out the Archbishop at Canterbury, pursued him into the Cathedral where his clergy had persuaded him to take refuge, and there murdered him in the heart of this own cathedral church. It was a crime which shocked Christendom. The four knights were excommunicated, and King Henry himself almost faced the same punishment. He escaped only by agreeing to undertake severe penances, and to abrogate those Constitutions of Clarendon which the pope had condemned. Thus Thomas won by his death what he had fought for in his life. The most dramatic sign of King Henry's penitence came on 12th July 1174, when he submitted to be scourged by the monks of Canterbury and spent a whole day and night at prayer before Thomas' tomb. But by that time Thomas had already been declared a martyr, and his heroism was celebrated at the altars of the Church. He is today the patron saint of the English secular clergy, and a fitting one, for as William Fitzstephen wrote: 'He was a good shepherd of

Christ's sheep, inasmuch as he laid down his life for them; archbishop and champion, confessor and martyr'.

RW

Places to Visit: The site of his martyrdom and original shrine in Canterbury Cathedral.

Further Reading:

Butler, J., *The Quest for Becket's Bones*, New Haven, Connecticut, Yale University Press, 1995.

Morris, J., *The Life and Martyrdom of Saint Thomas Becket*, London, Burns and Oates, 1885.

Reynolds, E. E., *St Thomas Becket*, CTS, 1970.

Winston, R., *Thomas Becket – Statesman, Soldier, Martyr and Saint*, New York, Alfred A. Knopf, 1967.

GENERAL FURTHER READING

Alton, D., *Pilgrim Ways*, St Paul's, 2001.

Attwater, D., *A Dictionary of Saints*, Burns, Oates & Washbourne, 1942.

St Bede the Venerable, *The Ecclesiastical History of the English People* (many editions).

Bowden, H., *Mementoes of the English Martyrs*, London, 1910.

Butler's Lives of the Saints (many editions).

Duffy, E., *The Stripping of the Altars*, Yale, 1992.

Farmer, D. H., *The Oxford Dictionary of Saints*, Oxford, Clarendon Press, 1978.

Newman, J. H. (ed.), *Newman's Lives of the British Saints*, London, 1900.

Purcell, J., *Pilgrim's England*, Longman, 1981.

Sherley-Price, L., *Saints of England*, London, 1936.

Stanton, A., *Menology of England and Wales*, London, Burns and Oates, 1887.

Ward, M. (ed.), *The English Way: Studies in English Sanctity from St Bede to Newman*, Sheed and Ward, 1934.

APPENDIX: SAINTS OF WALES

Other principal Welsh Saints and their feasts are listed below according to the Proper Calendar for Wales, 1981 (this calendar is only applicable to the dioceses of Wales)

St Teilo	9th February	Memorial
St David	1st March	Solemnity (Feast in England)
St Beuno	20th April	Optional Memorial
St Asaph	5th May	Optional Memorial
Sts Alban, Julius and Aaron	20th June	Memorial
St John Jones	12th July	Optional Memorial
Sts Philip Evans & John Lloyd	22nd July	Optional Memorial
St Germanus of Auxerre	3rd August	Optional Memorial
St David Lewis	26th August	Optional Memorial
St Deiniol	11th September	Optional Memorial
St Richard Gwyn	16th October	Memorial
Six Welsh Martyrs & Companions	25th October	Feast
St Winefride	3rd November	Optional Memorial (also in England)
St Illtud	6th November	Optional Memorial
All Saints of Wales	8th November	Feast
St Dyfrig	14th November	Optional Memorial
St John Roberts	10th December	Optional Memorial

These short biographical introductions to the Welsh Saints are drawn to a large extent from the compilations made by S. G. A. Luff and Byron Harries in the 1981 'Proper for Wales: a supplement to the Divine Office'.

ST TEILO

Teilo lived in the sixth century studying under St Paulinus at Llanddeusant and, as a monk, with St David at Mynyw. He founded his own monastery at Llandeilo Fawr where he probably died. A later tradition has St Teilo, accompanied by St David and St Padarn, make a pilgrimage to Jerusalem. He spent some years in Brittany. At Llandaff he is venerated as the founder of the see.

ST DAVID

See the full entry for 1st March earlier in this book.

ST BEUNO

St Beuno is venerated as the spiritual father of St Winefride, but he was also a monastic figure in the sixth century. He founded churches and monasteries, was noted for works of mercy, and died at Clynnog Fawr, where his shrine chapel is still a centre of devotion.

ST ASAPH

The little we know of St Asaph is found in the Life of St Kentigern, a bishop of Glasgow who in the seventh century founded a monastery in North Wales called Llanelwy, and later St Asaph. On his departure he instituted a beloved disciple, Asaph, bishop of a see ruled from the monastery. With some other Welsh communities, Llanelwy practised the 'Laus Perennis', a system of celebrating the Divine Office in relays so that worship was maintained without interruption.

STS ALBAN, JULIUS AND AARON

For St Alban, see the full entry above for 20th June. In the persecution of the Emperor Diocletian, Julius and Aaron at Caerleon-on-Usk are named among others who gave their lives for the faith.

ST JOHN JONES

He was a native of Clynnog Fawr near Caernarfon. He studied at the English College in Douai. After his ordination at Rheims in 1585 he returned to the English mission but was captured and imprisoned in Wisbech Castle. He either escaped or was released, and about 1592 made his profession as a Franciscan at the Convent of the Ara Coeli in Rome, taking the name Godfrey. He returned to the mission but after two years was arrested in Staffordshire, confined in the Marshalsea Prison, London, and finally executed in Southwark in 1598.

STS PHILIP EVANS AND JOHN LLOYD

Phillip Evans, born in Monmouth, became a Jesuit at Saint Omer and, after his ordination in 1675, ministered to Catholics in South Wales for four years. In the national frenzy occasioned by the Oates plot he was apprehended and imprisoned in Cardiff, where he was joined by John Lloyd of Brecon, a secular priest trained at Valladolid. They suffered the usual barbarous execution at Cardiff on 22nd July, 1679.

ST GERMANUS OF AUXERRE

Germanus was a bishop of Auxerre in Gaul who, according to St Bede the Venerable and other records, came as apostolic visitor to Britain in the early years of the fifth century to strengthen the Church in faith and practice. He is particularly noted for leading his British converts, newly baptised at Easter, in a bloodless victory over invading pagan forces, with 'Alleluia' as their cry. Early Lives of Saints revere Germanus as a founder of monastic life in Wales.

ST DAVID LEWIS

David Lewis' great uncle was Fr Augustine Baker, the Benedictine author of 'Holy Wisdom'. He was reconciled to the Church at the age of twenty, studied for the priesthood at the Venerable English College, Rome, and subsequently entered the Society of Jesus. For thirty years he laboured on the Hereford-Monmouth border where he became known as Father of the Poor. He was taken during the national scare occasioned by the Titus Oates plot, imprisoned at Monmouth and executed at Usk on 27th August, 1679, the last of the Welsh martyrs.

ST DEINIOL

Little is known of St Deiniol. He was a grandson of Pabo Post Prydyn, the British hero who renounced the world and died a hermit in Anglesey, and son of Dunawd, founder of the monastery of Bangor-on-Dee. He was himself founder of Bangor-in-Arfon, where tradition says he also became bishop. He was buried on Ynys Enlli – Bardsey Island.

ST RICHARD GWYN

Richard Gwyn was born in Llanidloes in Montgomeryshire and studied at Oxford and Cambridge. He became a schoolmaster in Wales and taught at Wrexham, Bangor-on-Dee, Gresford, Overton and Erbistock. Although he seems briefly to have conformed to the established religion, he was speedily reconciled to the Faith, imprisoned at Ruthin and Denbigh, and also at Bewdley in England, before his final trial and execution at Wrexham in 1584.

THE SIX WELSH MARTYRS & COMPANIONS

This is the specific feast of the six martyrs listed above and below and their many companions who died for the Catholic faith.

ST WINEFRIDE

See the full entry for 3rd November earlier in this book.

SAINT ILLTUD

St Illtud, who lived in the sixth century, was converted from a military career to a life of asceticism. He also became a famous teacher. His principal foundation was at Llanilltud Fawr, where he not only established an important school but ruled so large a community that it worshipped in relays, and so, like that at St Asaph in North Wales, practised the Laus Perennis. He is also credited with improving agricultural methods in Wales.

ALL SAINTS OF WALES

This feast celebrates all the saints listed here and otherwise who have graced Wales with their holiness.

ST DYFRIG

St Dyfrig was born in the sixth century in the Wye Valley, where he was also formed in the monastic life. At Moccas he founded a great monastery and rose to considerable influence as abbot and bishop. He is said to have received Illtud to repentance, to have ordained Samson to the priesthood, and to have consecrated Deiniol Bishop of Bangor. He resorted for prayer to Caldey Island, and in old age he retired to the island of Bardsey, where he died. Subsequently Bardsey became famous as the Island of Saints, and as a place of burial and pilgrimage.

ST JOHN ROBERTS

St John Roberts was born at Trawsfynnydd in Merioneth in 1576, made profession at the Benedictine Abbey of St Martin at Compostela in Spain, and was later founder and first prior of St Gregory's, Douai. He came several times to England as a missionary, and was finally captured in his Mass vestments in 1610. At Tyburn he proclaimed that he taught the same faith as did Augustine, Apostle of the English. He died with the venerable Thomas Somers, a secular priest.

INDEX OF SAINTS

ABOUT THE AUTHORS

Marcus Holden is a deacon of the archdiocese of Southwark. In 1995 he co-founded St Anthony Communications, an apostolate for the distribution of Catholic audio material and literature. He has theology degrees from Oxford University and the Pontifical Gregorian University. At present he lives in Rome at the Venerable English College and is pursuing a further licentiate degree in Patristics and the History of Theology. He was editor of the *Venerabile* journal (the official publication of the English College) between 2001 and 2003. He is due to be ordained priest in 2005.

Fr Nicholas Schofield is a priest of the Archdiocese of Westminster, currently serving at the Shrine of Our Lady of Willesden. He has a degree in Modern History from Exeter College, Oxford, and studied for the Priesthood at the Venerable English College, Rome. His published works include a history of the shrine of Our Lady of Willesden, which dates from the fifteenth century, and *A Roman Miscellany*, a collection of essays on Anglo-Roman history which he edited.

Fr Gerard Skinner. After studying at the Royal Academy of Music and two years as Organ Scholar at Westminster Cathedral, he went on to the Venerable English College in Rome as a seminarian for the Archdiocese of Westminster. He holds a licence in Dogmatic theology from the Pontifical Gregorian University. He was ordained to the priesthood in 2002 and is currently serving at the Church of St John the Evangelist, Islington.

Fr Richard Whinder studied History at Kings' College London. He trained for the Priesthood at the Venerable English College in Rome, and gained a Licence in Dogmatic Theology from the Pontifical Gregorian University. He was ordained Priest in 2001, and is currently an Assistant Priest in South London.